The Super Bowl

Sports Illustrated

The Super Bowl

SPORT'S GREATEST CHAMPIONSHIP

By Austin Murphy

SPORTS ILLUSTRATED is a
registered trademark of Time Inc.

ISBN 1-883013-41-0
Manufactured in the United States of America
First printing 1998

Library of Congress Catalog Card Number: 98-85734

Sports Illustrated Director of Development: STANLEY WEIL

THE SUPER BOWL
Project Director: MORIN BISHOP
  Senior Editors: JOHN BOLSTER, ANTHONY ZUMPANO,
EVE PETERSON
  Reporter: RACHAEL NEVINS
  Photography Editor: LAUREN CARDONSKY
Designers: BARBARA CHILENSKAS, JIA BAEK

THE SUPER BOWL was prepared by
Bishop Books, Inc.
611 Broadway
New York, New York 10012

Cover photograph (Terry Bradshaw):
NEIL LEIFER

TIME INC. HOME ENTERTAINMENT
President: DAVID GITOW
Director, Continuities and Single Sales: DAVID ARFINE
Director, Continuities and Retention: MICHAEL BARRETT
Director, New Products: ALICIA LONGOBARDO
Group Product Managers: ROBERT FOX, MICHAEL HOLAHAN
Product Managers: CHRISTOPHER BERZOLLA, ROBERTA HARRIS, STACY HIRSCHBERG,
  JENNIFER MCLYMAN, DANIEL MELORE
Manager, Retail and New Markets: THOMAS MIFSUD
Associate Product Managers: ALISON EHRMANN, CARLOS JIMENEZ, DARIA RAEHSE,
  BETTY SU, CHERYL ZUKOWSKI
Assistant Product Managers: MEREDITH SHELLEY, LAUREN ZASLANSKY
Editorial Operations Director: JOHN CALVANO
Fulfillment Director: MICHELLE GUDEMA
Assistant Fulfillment Manager: RICHARD PEREZ
Financial Director: TRICIA GRIFFIN
Associate Financial Manager: AMY MASELLI
Assistant Financial Manager: STEVEN SANDONATO
Marketing Assistant: ANN GILLESPIE

CONSUMER MARKETING DIVISION
Book Production Manager: JESSICA MCGRATH
Book Production Coordinator: JOSEPH NAPOLITANO

Special thanks to: ANNA YELENSKAYA

10 9 8 7 6 5 4 3 2 1

contents

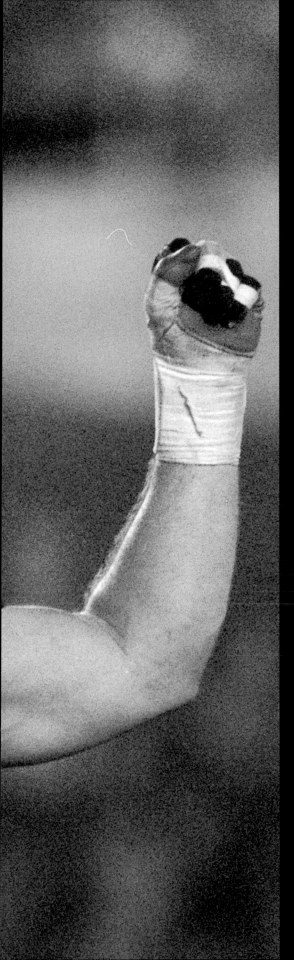

Introduction

Having delved into the archives, I stand ready to prognosticate. From Starr to Favre, from Too Tall to Mean Joe, from The Guarantee of Joe Namath to The Migraine of Terrell Davis, I have steeped myself in the lore of our unofficial national holiday. If past is prologue, I predict the following for future Super Bowls:

• It will come to light on a future Super Sunday that the winning team was somehow not accorded sufficient respect; was disrespected, a.k.a. "dissed."

There was the Denver Broncos' plainspoken linebacker Bill Romanowski, for example, confessing on national television in the moments after his team's upset of Green Bay in Super Bowl XXXII, that the pregame hype surrounding the defending champs "made me wanna puke."

Despite their 16–0 record in 1972, the Miami Dolphins were underdogs to the Washington Redskins in Super Bowl VII. Following the 14–7 victory which gave them an unprecedented 17–0 season, the Dolphins could finally feel respected. After those teams met again in Supe XVII in 1983 and the Redskins won

Amidst his joyful celebration after Super Bowl XXXII, Romanowski (left) took time out to offer his trenchant analysis of the pregame hype.

Bill Walsh (above) participated in a typically inane bit of banter with President Reagan after Super Bowl XVI; Vince Ferragamo (right) gave a solid performance in a losing cause in XIV but missed the mark with his prediction of a return engagement.

27–17, Washington coach Joe Gibbs declared, "Maybe now we'll get all the respect we deserve."

In his heart of hearts, no coach ever wants his team to get the full measure of respect it deserves. To earn that is to lose a perfectly good motivational tool.

• A future Super Sunday will feature a deafening and irrelevant halftime show, which brazenly proclaims its wretched excess with the slogan "Up With People."

• Some defensive back will pop off during the weeks leading up to a future Super Bowl, then get burned repeatedly during the game. The futile attempts by Dallas Cowboys safety Cliff Harris to intimidate Lynn Swann before Supes X and XIII spring to mind, as does the bluster of Kansas City Chiefs cornerback Fred Williamson, who took pleasure in meting out his patented "hammer"—a forearm chop to the helmet. In the days before the inaugural Super Bowl, Williamson promised to drop the hammer on Green Bay's receivers.

As it turned out, they were too busy catching Bart Starr's passes in front of him to give the hammer much mind. In the fourth quarter, Williamson was run over and

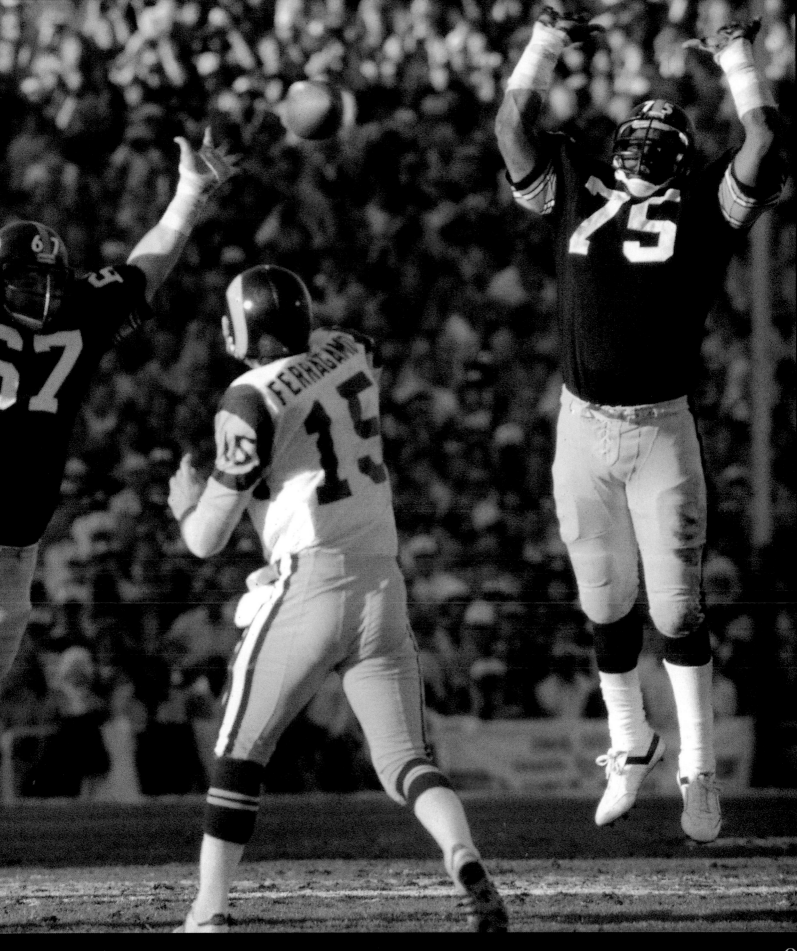

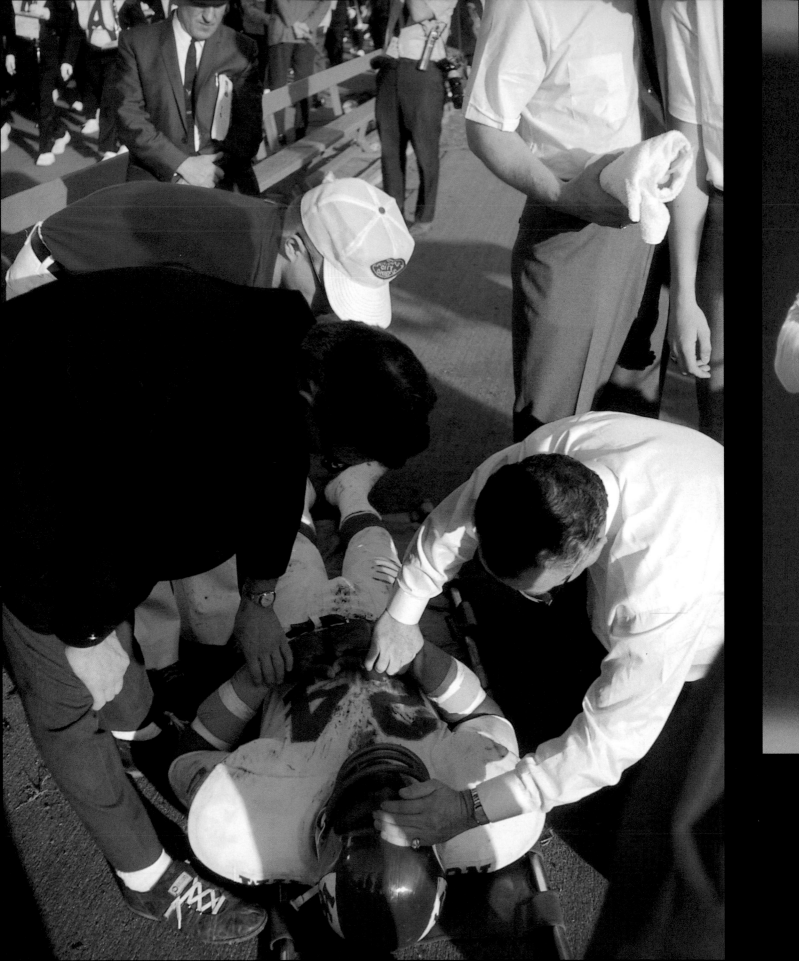

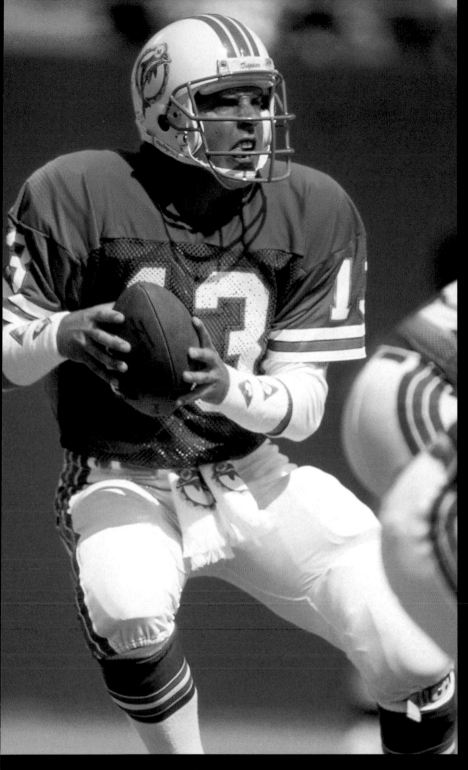

and forced bonhomie, such as this gem between Ronald Reagan and Bill Walsh after Supe XVI in 1982:

RR: "You might tell Joe Montana and the fellows that they really did win one for the Gipper."

BW: "I think Joe was thinking of the Gipper when he won that one. Thank you very much."

Reagan had no idea that the "fellows" weren't all that happy with him at the time, since a traffic jam in Pontiac, Mich., created by his vice president George Bush's motorcade had almost caused them to miss the kickoff.

Just once we would like to hear a candid exchange in this traditional phone call, a head coach willing to tell the chief executive, "About that bill you vetoed last week—I just wanted to let you know how gutless I thought that was."

• Someone in the losers' locker room will lift his chin and—in a tone reprising Arnold Schwarzenegger's Terminator vow, "I'll be back"—predict a return trip. After Supe XXXI, New England Patriots quarterback Drew Bledsoe told me, "We're so young, if we can stay healthy and learn from this, we can get back here."

Bledsoe could not have known that he was echoing the vow of Los Angeles Rams quarterback Vince Ferragamo, who said, "We're young. We'll be back," after losing to the Steelers in Supe XIV.

In hindsight, these bluff predictions contain a certain poignance. They are often inaccurate, and serve to underscore the damnable elusiveness of this goal. To

knocked unconscious by rookie running back Donny Anderson. Just before Williamson was stretchered off the field, the story goes, Packers guard Fuzzy Thurston stood over him, quietly humming the song "If I Had a Hammer."

• The President of the United States and the winning coach will have a phone conversation following a future Super Bowl that will be characterized by inanity

play in the Super Bowl, let alone win it, requires equal measures of talent and good fortune. Ask Dan Marino, who made it to the Super Bowl in 1985 after his second season, but hasn't been back. This is a game played in front of the world and on top of a vast pyramid. Those who play in it, whose stories are recounted here, comprise the lucky few.

FIRST QUARTER:

the games

The Games

Vince Lombardi must share the blame. His dynastic Green Bay Packers set an unfortunate precedent when they won the first two Super Bowls by a combined score of 68–24. Whether it was the Miami Dolphins crushing the Minnesota Vikings 24–7 in Super Bowl VIII or the Denver Broncos getting waxed by a combined 108–40 in Super Bowls XII, XXI and XXII, or the God-help-us-not-them-again Buffalo Bills going belly up four straight times, all blowouts save the first one, from XXV to XXVIII; somewhere along the line those Roman numerals became synonymous with slaughter.

We're not cheerleaders here. We're not saying there haven't been some mutt games. But the perception of the Super Bowl as a Super Bore is one that has been blown out of proportion. But then, what aspect of this unofficial national holiday isn't writ large? Namath's guarantee (III), Swann's acrobatics (X), Montana's 11-play dissection of the Bengals (XXIII), Elway's leap (XXXII)—each of these moments has been transformed into something, if not larger than life, then at least as massive as Bill Parcells's ego. It's the magnitude of the occasion that does it: the massive hype, the worldwide audience, the championship on the line. The stakes can't get any higher. Unless of course you do something reckless, like publicly guarantee that your side will win.

While selecting the Top Ten Super Bowls, we threw some pretty good ones overboard. Baltimore's 16–13 win over the Cowboys in Super Bowl V, won by a rookie kicker named Jim O'Brien, came down to the wire, but with 11 turnovers—*Sports Illustrated* dubbed it the Blunder Bowl—it was too sloppy to rate as a great one. Likewise Dallas's 27–17 win over the Steelers in Super Bowl XXX, which the Cowboys didn't so much win as have handed to them by Pitts-

O'Brien's game-winning kick (left) almost put Super Bowl V on our list, but 11 turnovers were too many to overlook.

Jim Kelly (left) was the hapless leader of the God-help-us-not-them-again Bills, who fell in four straight Super Bowls; Elway (right) redeemed his years of Super futility with his dramatic leap in XXXII.

burgh quarterback Neil O'Donnell, who threw three interceptions, two of them particularly egregious.

Now, at the end of the century, we're on a roll. Super Bowls XXX, XXXI and XXXII were each not decided until well into the fourth quarter. Nary an anticlimax among them. In what we are calling the Best Super Bowl Ever—which is to say, The Very Good Super Bowl That Is Freshest In Our Memories— Denver's triumph over Green Bay in XXXII snapped an ugly 0–4 Super streak for the Broncos and an uglier 0–13 stretch for the American Football Conference. With the AFC off the schneid, and with an NFL salary cap and free-agency system in place that prevents teams from staying too good for too long, we foresee a new era of taut, dramatic Super Bowls.

What the hell, let's borrow a page from Namath's playbook. We guarantee it.

denver **Broncos** 31
green bay **Packers** 24

SUPER BOWL XXXII JANUARY 25, 1998

After 15 pro campaigns and three crushing Super Bowl defeats, Elway (left) and his Broncos, betting underdogs but sentimental favorites, emerged triumphant on the final day of the NFL season.

The game was still several days away, and already the talk about long-suffering Denver quarterback John Elway had begun to wear out certain Green Bay Packers. "We've all heard about poor John Elway," said defensive tackle Santana Dotson. "We're all very touched."

Dotson's dis was a reminder that No. 7 of the Denver Broncos was despised in certain parts of the country: AFC West cities, mainly, and Cleveland. Most of the country, however, had come to know him for what he was, a good person with a ready smile, loads of talent and a small but significant gap in his resume. This Bronco was saddled with America's most famous 0-fer.

As in, 0 for 3—three Super Bowl appearances, three lopsided defeats. So there was nationwide cringing when the Broncos beat the Steelers in the AFC championship and earned the right to play Green Bay in Super Bowl XXXII in San Diego. With another disaster surely impending—Denver was a double-digit

'dog to the defending champions—friends of Elway fought the urge to look away. It was as if Mr. Bill had decided, one final time, to trust Sluggo.

Given the histories of the Broncos and their conference—the AFC had lost the previous 13 Super Bowls—Denver seemed strangely confident going into the game. It started with head coach Mike Shanahan, who said to a reporter more than a week before the game, "With all the hype Green Bay's getting, the whole AFC inferiority thing, everybody will be stroking them. It will all work in our favor, and our guys are pretty determined."

Indeed, after allowing a touchdown on Green Bay's first possession, the Broncos responded with a pair of TD drives to go ahead 14–7, and answered the weighty question: How would Denver's offensive line—the NFL's lightest, at an anemic average of 289 pounds per man—fare against the celebrated Green Bay front four which featured future Hall of Famer Reggie White and credenza-sized noseguard Gilbert Brown?

Denver's undersized hogs were more than up to the task. Brown, playing at least 30 pounds over his listed weight of 345, was sucking carpet tacks all day. White had one tackle, on Denver's second play, then disappeared. Despite missing virtually the entire second quarter with the symptoms of a nascent migraine, Broncos run-

Where's the beef? The Broncos' NFL-lite offensive line dominated the meaty Packers defensive front, allowing MVP Davis (above) to gallop for 157 yards and three touchdowns in barely three quarters of play.

ning back Terrell Davis slashed through the Green Bay defense for 157 yards, three touchdowns and one MVP award.

With apologies to T.D., the game's most memorable rush belonged to his 37-year-old teammate. With the score tied 17–17 in the third quarter, Elway bolted the pocket on a third-and-six at the Green Bay 12-yard line, leapt and was smacked in midair by Packers safety LeRoy Butler. After helicoptering back to the turf, having picked up the first down, Elway got up pumping his fist. "It energized us beyond

belief," said defensive tackle Mike Lodish.

Denver's D would need that energy for one final stand. Leading 31–24 with 1:39 left, they faced Green Bay quarterback Brett Favre, who was determined to lead a game-winning drive. Favre had thrown three touchdown passes in the game but was never able to settle into a rhythm. He had to contend with an uncharacteristically exotic mix of blitzes thrown at him by the Broncos. That package included an eight-man rush on Green Bay's last gasp, a fourth-and-six play from the

Denver 31 with 32 seconds remaining. Favre's pass, broken up by linebacker John Mobley, hit the turf, incomplete. Elway took one snap, knelt, and a career's frustrations were erased.

No one in the Elway family seemed sure of how to proceed in the wake of a victory on the season's final day. "I only know to handle a loss in these," admitted John's wife, Janet. Jack Elway, so often his son's post–Super Bowl grief counselor, clinched his son in a long, tight, joyous embrace.

Santana Dotson himself would have found it touching.

BY RICK REILLY (02/04/98)

So far in Elway's career, his offensive linemen and wide receivers have been voted to the Pro Bowl a combined seven times. In Dan Marino's 15 seasons, Miami Dolphins offensive linemen and wide receivers have been selected to the Pro Bowl 30 times.... Though usually surrounded by a human rummage sale, Elway has won more games as a starter than any other quarterback in NFL history (138). It's the equivalent of carving Mount Rushmore with a spoon or composing Beethoven's Ninth on a kazoo.

But Elway's career has been about more than just winning. It has been about escaping defeat a half page from the end of the novel, leaping over pits of fire with the microdot hidden in his cigarette lighter. On first down Elway was "pretty average," his Stanford coach Paul Wiggin once said. But when the elementary school kids are being held hostage and the detonator reads 00:03, who would you rather have clipping the wires than Elway? He may be the only quarterback in history who could stand on his own two-yard line, trailing by five with less than two minutes to play, no timeouts left, windchill −5, and cause the opposing coach to mutter, "We're in trouble."

Favre (below) and the Packers, in search of back-to-back titles, were kept off balance throughout the game by a dazzling array of Denver defensive sets.

new york **Giants 20**

buffalo **Bills 19**

SUPER BOWL XXV JANUARY 27, 1991

This was the league that said "Play ball!" two days after the assassination of President John F. Kennedy. Obviously, the NFL wasn't going to let a two-bit tyrant like Saddam Hussein interfere with the Silver Anniversary of its showcase event. Concessions, however, had to be made to the conflict in the Persian Gulf. Security for Super Bowl XXV was ratcheted up several notches. Spectators filing in to Tampa Stadium had to pass through specially constructed concrete barriers and metal detectors, whereupon they were nosed by bomb-sniffing dogs.

The game they watched was hardly less tense, with the outcome in doubt until a missed field goal with four seconds on the clock. Poor Scott Norwood, the Buffalo Bills kicker, earned an eternity in goat's horns for his infamous wide right. Ottis Anderson, the New York Giants' minitank of a running back, was voted the game's MVP for grinding out 102 unglamorous yards rushing.

But the most important player in this wartime Super Bowl was Jeff Hostetler, who was as much foot soldier as quarterback.

A clipboard caddy for 6½ of his first seven NFL seasons, Hoss had been thrust into the starting lineup six weeks earlier, when starting quarterback Phil Simms suffered a badly sprained right foot in a game against the Bills. Fortunately for Hoss, New York's ground-bound offense was one of the NFL's more primitive attacks. And Giants head coach Bill Parcells believed in Hostetler. "Jeff Hostetler can do the job," he said.

Not if he was unconscious, he couldn't. One of the drawbacks of the brontosaurian offensive linemen favored by Parcells was that they were not the most nimble of pass-blockers. The first half of Super Bowl XXV saw the erstwhile backup absorb shot after bone-jarring shot. After getting his world rocked in the second quarter by Bills end Leon Seals, Hostetler was given an ammonia cap to sniff. On the next series he was mauled in the Giants' end zone by Buffalo defensive end Bruce Smith for a safety that put the Bills up 12–3.

Woozy though he may have been, Hoss did what he had to do: sustain drives and eat clock. Buffalo's newfangled, no-huddle offense had scored 51 points on the Oakland Raiders in their first playoff game, then rang up 44 more on the

Norwood's miss launched four straight years of Super Bowl futility for the Buffalo Bills; the results would only get more lopsided.

A big cog in the Giants' clock-controlling machine was MVP Anderson, whose 34-year-old legs churned out 102 yards, including this one-yard score that put the Giants up 17–12 in the third quarter.

Despite taking a pounding, Hoss was Boss, scrambling repeatedly to convert third-down situations and keep the Giants' drives alive.

Miami Dolphins a week later. Behind Hostetler, the Giants did a masterful job of bogarting the ball and keeping Bills quarterback Jim Kelly off the field. When the game was over, following Norwood's ill-fated 47-yard field goal attempt, the Giants had kept the ball for a whopping 40 minutes and 33 seconds, a Super Bowl record.

When the Bills did have the ball, they were often confounded by the innovations of Giants defensive coordinator Bill Belichick, who crowded Kelly's passing zones with three or four linebackers and five or six defensive backs. Reyna Thompson, normally a special teams commando, was inserted into the defensive backfield with the task of funnelling wideout Andre Reed toward the linebackers. The Giants' linebackers allowed Reed to run his beloved crossing routes, but exacted a steep toll. "No other team ever hit me this hard," said Reed after the game. "They bruised up my whole body."

Did Belichick's schemes work?

Kelly didn't convert a third-down play until less than two minutes remained. Yet there the Bills were—thanks in large part to the brilliance of running back Thurman Thomas, who broke off a 31-yard TD ramble to give the Bills a 19–17 fourth-quarter lead—lining up for what would have been the game winning field-goal with four seconds left.

Afterward, in New York's locker room, Ron Hostetler asked his brother, "How do you feel?"

"Still a little woozy," said Jeff. "Pretty bad headache right now." On his right temple, courtesy of Seals, was an ugly bruise. A purple welt ran the length of his left side. The headache was not soothed by a visit from linebacker Pepper Johnson, who led a group of Giants in a chant at Hostetler's locker.

"You can't do it! You can't do it!" the Giants chanted. "They say you're a backup! You can't do it!"

Hostetler smiled. The backup knew better.

postgame

However much responsibility Scott Norwood truly bears for the Bills' loss in Super Bowl XXV, his name will forever be linked with the crushing defeat. You'd think his last-second miss of a 47-yard field-goal attempt was a gaffe as glaring as Viking Jim Marshall's famous wrong-way fumble return against the 49ers in 1964. Remember, this was a 47-yard attempt. Hardly a chip shot. If the Bills had managed the clock better during their final possession, Norwood might have been closer to the uprights for his all-or-nothing kick. As it was, he missed by two feet. Following the Bills' 37–24 loss to Washington in the next Super Bowl, he was released by the team. Unable to catch on with another NFL team, Norwood returned to his native Virginia, where he started a family with his wife, Kim, and got into the insurance business. "A lot of people thought my life was ruined, but nothing could be further from the truth," Norwood said some seven years after The Miss. "Sure, I wish I had made that kick, but my life didn't go into a tailspin."

san francisco **49ers 20**

cincinnati **Bengals 16**

It was one of the great salvage jobs of all time. For nearly 45 minutes this game had the look of a bust, a dud championship on the heels of a disastrous week in south Florida. On the Monday night preceding Super Bowl XXIII, a policeman shot and killed a black motorcyclist in the Overtown section of Miami, triggering 48 hours of arson, looting and riots. Not exactly the backdrop the NFL had sought for its title game.

A 3–3 first half wasn't exactly the ticket, either. But after the third quarter, the game came alive. San Francisco quarterback Joe Montana gave the NFL a gift it had been awaiting nearly a quarter century—the spectacle of the league's best quarterback taking over its biggest game at the most critical time. When it could not have mattered more, Montana found ... Uncle Buck?

"Hey," said Joe Cool as the Niners huddled, trailing 16–13 with the clock winding down, "there's John Candy." The rotund comedian was indeed in Miami's Joe Robbie Stadium that night. Nice of Montana to point him out for his teammates. The best quarterback ever then deftly took the spotlight off the riots and put it back on the game.

Rumors had swirled throughout the week that the NFL would have to amend the rules to slow the Bengals' postmodern, no-huddle offense because it gave Cincinnati an unfair advantage. They could put teams on the ropes by running play after play without allowing the defense time to adjust. But on this Sunday, the no-huddle offense was the no-touchdown offense. Pressured and perplexed by a mix of blitzes and varying coverages, Bengals quarterback Boomer Esiason completed just 11 of 25 passes for 144 yards.

The entire Bengals squad, it seemed, came into the game off balance. From their rooms at the Omni International Hotel in downtown Miami, they were able to see Overtown burning. On the eve of the game, Cincinnati fullback Stanley Wilson was found in his room, out of his head on cocaine. The league was informed, and Stanley was given the next day off.

Wilson's sad lapse meant more playing time for Stanford Jennings, who jump-started a dull game with a 93-yard kickoff return in the waning seconds

Taylor made his first catch of the game count, hauling in Montana's 10-yard pass for the touchdown that put the 49ers ahead for good.

of the third quarter. Cincinnati had the lead, 13–6, and the Super Bowl, as we remember it, could begin.

The suddenly no-nonsense Montana drove the 49ers offense 85 yards in the next 91 seconds. That efficient, four-play march—ending in a balletic touch-down reception by Jerry Rice—tied the game but turned out to be only an hors d'oeuvre, a prelude to The Drive.

Cincinnati kicker Jim Breech gave his team a 16–13 lead with his third field goal of the day, and the 49ers were penalized back to their eight-yard line on the ensuing kickoff. The game clock read 3:10; the Niners had three time-outs. On the Bengals sideline, some simpleton shouted, "We got 'em!"

The Drive started unspectacularly. Three snaps resulted in three short Montana completions to a trio of receivers. Dinks gave way to intermediate passes: a 17-yarder to Rice, a 13-yarder to Roger Craig. When time is short, you work the sidelines—so says conventional football wisdom. Montana

Despite a swollen ankle, Rice had an MVP day, catching 11 passes for a Super Bowl–record 215 yards.

Montana's confidence in the huddle was matched by his poise in the pocket as he marched the Niners 97 yards in 2:36 to complete The Drive.

worked the middle, "right where our strength wasn't," lamented Bengals cornerback Lewis Billups. Another daring completion between the hashes—27 yards to Rice—followed by a dump-off to Craig, set up 20 Halfback Curl X-Up.

That was Montana's call following his celebrity sighting, with :39 left. The Niners had the ball, second-and-two on the 10. Wideout John Taylor, who did not have a catch in the game, lined up as a tight end on the left side. Rice went in motion to that side, forcing Bengals safety Ray Horton to cheat toward the sideline. "Before I could react," recalled Horton, "the ball was in the air."

Taylor's first catch of the game was the most memorable of his career, and won for the 49ers their third NFL title of the decade. Montana had salvaged a Super Bowl, for his team and for the league. Said 49ers center Randy Cross, "Anybody who thought Joe Montana had a peer might reconsider that now."

in SI's words

RALPH WILEY (1/30/89)

Jerry Rice wanted to be alone. So he separated himself from the crowd and slipped smoothly off the field and into the locker room. Then he walked over to a row of lockers and started crying with such deep-felt emotion he had to bend over to control his tears. Finally, after a few moments, he lifted his head, smiled and joined his teammates in the postgame revelry.

Rice, the San Francisco 49ers' extraordinary wide receiver, had reason to be emotional. He had just caught 11 passes from Joe Montana, including one 14-yard touchdown grab, and would soon be named MVP of Super Bowl XXIII.

But what set him apart was the manner in which he caught those passes and the vistas he opened for others to catch what he couldn't. "We didn't do a bad job on him," said Cincinnati Bengal strong safety David Fulcher. "He only got one touchdown." When you gain a record 215 yards receiving in the Super Bowl and the defense doesn't think it has done a bad job, you must be a different breed of cat.

new york **Jets 16**

baltimore **Colts 7**

SUPER BOWL III JANUARY 12, 1969

Sharing the front page of *The New York Times* on Jan. 13, 1969, along with an incredulous account of the greatest upset in pro football history, was a story about the ongoing, smooth transition between President-elect Richard Nixon and outgoing President Lyndon Johnson. A nation, and a sport, were in flux.

Gotham's tabloids referred to football's main agent of change as a "playboy" and "sideburned swinger." There was no mistaking New York Jets quarterback Joe Namath for Earl Morrall, his crewcut counterpart in Super Bowl III. While Namath represented football's counterculture, Morrall and his Baltimore Colts, coached by the jut-jawed Don Shula, stood for the status quo—which suited them just fine. Before the Jets shocked Baltimore, 16–7, the NFL had yet to lose a Super Bowl.

Even though Morrall had led the Colts to 15 wins in 16 games that season, Namath couldn't resist tossing a dart his way: He estimated the upstart AFL had at least four quarterbacks better than old Earl. "And I'm one of 'em," said Broadway Joe.

Audacity made its masterpiece three nights before the game, when Namath, addressing an awards banquet and clutching a double-scotch, guaranteed a win over the Colts. While his smack-talking might seem mild by today's less civil standards, three decades ago it simply wasn't done. It rankled the proud Colts, who had won 28 of their previous 30 games. Defensive tackle Billy Ray Smith warned that Namath should "keep his mouth shut" because "he'll keep his teeth longer."

Playboy and party animal though he may have been, Namath was no idiot. After putting on an impressive pregame show, lofting bomb after bomb into the afternoon air at the Orange Bowl, he all but abandoned the long ball, subjecting the vaunted Colts defense to a death by a thousand cuts. None of the 17 passes Namath completed (in 28 attempts) was longer than 39 yards. And while he was named the game's MVP for the savvy he showed in recognizing blitzes and throwing zero interceptions—and, let's face it, for being Broadway Joe—the trophy could have gone to Jets running back Matt Snell, who rushed for 121 yards

Namath's right arm spoke as loudly during the game as his mouth did before it, producing 206 passing yards en route to the upset win over the Colts.

RICK TELANDER (9/19/94)

Once upon a time, Joe Namath had good knees.... University of Alabama head coach Bear Bryant called him "the greatest athlete I have ever coached." But the knee injuries came in rapid succession toward the end of Namath's Alabama career, and the surgeries followed, and the brash, working-class quarterback from Beaver Falls, Pa., quickly metamorphosed into that most poignant of icons, the young, wounded hero....

When the Jets stunned the Colts with their 16–7 Super Bowl victory, they shocked America, too. Underdogs everywhere rejoiced. Overdogs licked their wounds and reexamined their status; not the least of these was the NFL, which just four months later agreed to merge with the once-scorned AFL. The legend of Joe Namath, meanwhile, was guaranteed, forever disguising the fact that Namath, in his 13-year pro career, would play on just four plus-.500 teams. He peaked and faded fast. Wounded heroes do that....

As his agent Jimmy Walsh predicted almost 20 years ago, "Eventually, Joe Namath the football player will not be as significant as the idea of him." For a while there, though, the idea was real. And wild as can be.

Some of the credit for the win must go to Jets coach Weeb Ewbank (left) whose conservative game plan turned the air-it-out AFL's gambling image on its head.

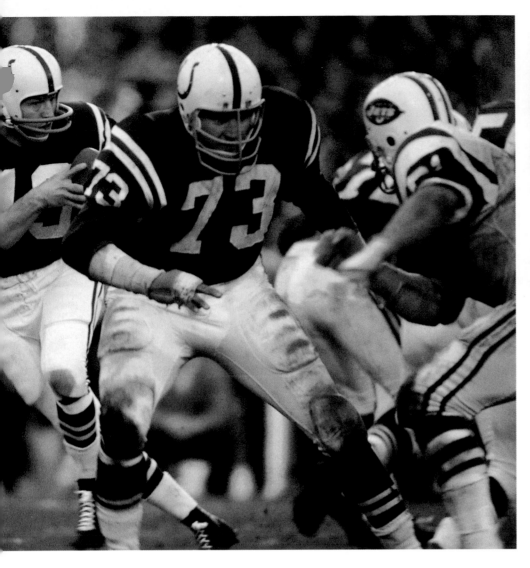

Unitas (left) couldn't summon
any last-minute magic; Namath's
postgame declaration (above)
matched his pregame prediction.

and chose an opportune Sunday to turn in a career performance.

As the game unfolded, stereotypes about the fast-and-loose AFL and the staid NFL faded into irrelevance. New York's sole touchdown came in the second quarter on a methodical, 12-play drive which got off to a Lombardian start, with four Snell carries for 26 yards. While the Jets kept the favorites off balance, mixing pass and run, it was the formerly tackle-to-tackle Colts who were forced to resort to gadgetry. On the last play of the first half, Morrall called a flea-flicker. It should have worked. After handing off to running back Tom Matte, who lateraled the ball back to him, Morrall had receiver Jimmy Orr alone near the goal line. "I did everything but shoot up a flare," the forlorn Orr would later report. But Morrall didn't see him. His pass to fullback Jerry Hill was picked off by Jets defensive back Jim Hudson.

Morrall was intercepted three times, after which Shula called his backup, the sore-armed, 35-year-old Johnny Unitas, to save Baltimore's bacon. And while Unitas prevented a shutout, leading the Colts to one window-dressing touchdown, this was Namath's day.

Before an estimated television audience of 70 million people, the 25-year-old bachelor from Beaver Falls, Pa., demonstrated that the older league did not have a monopoly on football excellence. To express it in today's trash-talk parlance, Namath had "walked the walk," and immeasurably strengthened the Super Bowl in the process.

In the losers' locker room, a veteran Colt was asked what he thought of Namath now. "He gets my vote," said Billy Ray Smith. The kid was all right.

green bay **Packers 35**

new england **Patriots 21**

If you judged solely by the pregame hype, you might have thought only two people were involved in Super Bowl XXXI at the Louisiana Superdome: Green Bay Packers quarterback Brett Favre and New England Patriots head coach Bill Parcells. The Gregarious Mississippian vs. the Pear-Shaped Master Motivator for all the marbles.

But in the game that brought the Vince Lombardi Trophy back home for the first time since 1968, the spotlight was stolen, perhaps appropriately, by a return specialist. The Pack had jumped out to an early 10–0 lead—and given millions of television viewers reason to believe that another Super Rout was underway—but then couldn't put the pesky Patriots away.

That was left to former University of Michigan star and Heisman Trophy winner Desmond Howard. Even before New England had narrowed the Packers' lead to 27–21 late in the third quarter, the Green Bay kick returner had made his mark on the game: His punt returns

of 32 and 34 yards had led to 10 Green Bay points. Now, with 3:10 left in the third quarter, the 5'9" 180-pound Howard hurtled into a fissure in the Patriots' kickoff coverage and emerged in the far end zone. His 99-yard touchdown turned a tight contest into a convincing, 35–21 Packers victory.

"Until that point," Parcells said of Howard's back-breaking runback, "I thought we still had an opportunity to win." The Tuna would resign several days later and eventually take the New York Jets' head coaching job. The vast media attention Parcells generated in New Orleans created a distraction for his team and raised the ire of the Packers. "Parcells, Parcells, Parcells," griped Green Bay strong safety LeRoy Butler on the eve of the game. "I know [he] wants attention, but next time he should have more respect for [Packers head coach Mike Holmgren]."

One player who didn't seem to mind the focus on the Tuna was Favre, who was quite happy to let controversy swirl around someone else for a change. The talkative quarterback had dropped a bombshell on the sports world the previous spring, announcing that he would enter a rehab facility for addiction to a painkiller. Favre followed his 6½-week stint in the clinic with his second straight MVP season.

After all he had been through, Favre's championship season was nearly derailed on the Thursday night before the game when he was laid low by the

Howard's heroics, including a dramatic 99-yard kickoff return, sealed the Packers' win and earned the former Heisman winner the MVP award.

Favre (opposite) complemented Green Bay's solid rushing game by completing 14 of his 27 passing attempts for 246 yards and two touchdowns, including a 54-yarder to Rison (left) which put the Pack in front 7–0.

postgame

The news following Super Bowl XXXI was less about the game than about the future of Bill Parcells, who resigned as Patriots coach on January 31, 1997. His contract prevented him from taking another head coaching job with another NFL team for one season, but the Jets—who were looking for a savior after consecutive seasons of 3–13 and 1–15 under Rich Kotite—thought they had found a loophole by hiring Parcells as a "consultant" and giving the coaching headset to longtime Parcells assistant Bill Belichick.

Patriots owner Robert Kraft labeled the arrangement a "transparent farce" and demanded the Jets' No. 1 pick in the upcoming draft as restitution. The NFL stepped in and brokered a deal which gave New England the Jets' third- and fourth-round picks in 1997, their second-round pick in 1998, and their first-round pick in 1999, while allowing Parcells to take over as Jets coach for the 1997 season.

The results? In 1997–98, the Jets finished 9–7, their best record since 1986, and barely missed the playoffs. The Patriots hired Pete Carroll—who had coached the Jets before Kotite's disastrous turn—and he led New England to a 10–6 record, the AFC East title, and a second-round playoff loss to Pittsburgh.

flu. Did he make a full recovery? The question might be better answered by Otis Smith, the Patriots corner whom Favre roasted on Green Bay's second play from scrimmage. Suspecting an all-out blitz, Favre audibled out of 322 Y Stick—a quick out to tight end Mark Chmura—to 74 Razor, which called for Andre Rison to run a deep post. Rison gathered in Favre's pass five yards clear of Smith, and duckwalked into the end zone.

Howard, too, slowed down to a showboating walk before scoring his dramatic TD. Noticing this as he watched a replay during the presentation of the MVP award to Howard, the returner's agent, Leigh Steinberg, clucked disapprovingly. He didn't want his client coming off like a hot dog. "In an endorsement sense," the über-agent said, "this MVP can be worth millions."

Howard did strike it rich, bolting Green Bay to sign a multimillion dollar deal with the Oakland Raiders, with whom he has struggled. Green Bay's brass gave the impression of only mild regret at Howard's departure. In his lone season as a Packer, though, Howard had delivered precisely what Cheeseheads hoped he would: many happy returns.

pittsburgh **Steelers 21**
dallas **Cowboys 17**

If he has it to do over again, maybe Dallas offensive tackle Rayfield Wright thanks the exotic dancer and accepts her good luck charm. If he has it to do over again, maybe Cowboys safety Cliff Harris concentrates on the game, rather than trying to go spelunking inside Pittsburgh wide receiver Lynn Swann's head.

The ham-handed attempts of Harris to intimidate Swann back fired as spectacularly as Swann performed. In this tenth Super Bowl, it was Swann's four catches for 161 yards and one touchdown that pushed Pittsburgh over the top.

Swann had been cold-cocked a fortnight earlier in the AFC title game by a clothesline tackle courtesy of Oakland Raiders safety George Atkinson. The concussion Swann suffered on the play was his second of the season and resulted in a two-day hospital stay. During Super Bowl week Harris repeatedly suggested that if Swann valued what remaining brain cells he had, he'd think twice about coming over the middle.

The unusually high level of antipathy between these two teams was based on genuine philosophical differences. The Cowboys' offense was predicated on deception: It relied on the shotgun formation, and sent more men in motion than a Village People concert. And Dallas's renowned "Flex" defense—with linemen setting up at odd angles, sometimes a yard off the ball—was designed to slip the traps that were a staple of the Steelers' running game. The emphasis on trickery annoyed the defending champs. "To me," said Steelers defensive tackle Mean Joe Greene, "football is executing, just blocking and tackling better, not fooling people."

Near the end of the first half, after hooking wide a 36-yard field-goal attempt that would have tied the game, Steelers kicker Roy Gerela got a pat on the head from that dime-store psychiatrist, Harris. This patronizing act sat well with neither the kicker's simian fan club, Gerela's Gorillas, nor with snaggle-toothed middle linebacker Jack Lambert, who seemed to be saying, as he body-slammed the insolent Harris, *You can't do that to our kicker—only we can do that to our kicker.*

Harris continued to woof at Swann during the game. Because Swann stood a mere 5'11" and weighed 180 pounds, had studied ballet, dabbled in poetry and had a feminine first name, it was easy to underestimate the amount of steel in this Steeler. But Harris, and the rest of the world, discovered that you underestimated Swann at your own peril, as the Pittsburgh receiver made three of the most

Swann's dazzling acrobatics, including this bobbling grab for 53 yards, produced gasps of amazement from the crowd and an MVP award for Swann.

Bradshaw completed just nine passes but still threw for 209 yards, including a record 161 to Swann.

memorable catches in Super Bowl history on this crisp afternoon in the Orange Bowl.

The first was the most jaw-dropping. Swann's contorted, skywalking stab of a 32-yard sideline pass in the first quarter defied the laws of physics, as did his ability to seemingly change direction, mid-flight, and get both feet in bounds. This was the key play in Pittsburgh's first TD drive. The catch you remember, the catch everyone remembers, was squandered. Shortly after Swann bobbled a 53-yard pass from Terry Bradshaw, then reeled it in from a prone

position, Gerela pulled that field goal attempt. Dallas held a 10–7 lead when the teams broke for halftime.

The Cowboys were about to punt early in the fourth quarter when an exotic dancer named Bambi Brown ran onto the field and handed Wright a silver horseshoe good-luck charm. He threw it away, and would later say, "Maybe I should have hung on to it."

Bad juju for Dallas? In rapid order, this happened: An obscure running back named Reggie Harrison blocked the ensuing punt with his face. The ball caromed out of the end zone for a safety.

Gerela nailed a pair of field goals, and Swann came up with one last gorgeous catch, a 64-yard bomb for a touchdown which Bradshaw released one nanosecond before Dallas defensive tackle Larry Cole knocked him cold. Swann's score made it Steelers 21, Cowboys 10.

Dallas scored a final TD but was one big play shy of victory. With the game over, did these two teams finally put their differences behind them? Not exactly. "The really unfortunate thing," said Dallas tight end Jean Fugett, "is that that team of asses is the world champions."

When not chasing Bradshaw and Swann, the Cowboys faced the rushing tandem of Harris (below) and Rocky Bleier, who combined for 133 yards.

DAN JENKINS (1/26/76)

That last catch of Swann's has to be dwelled on. There was so much to the play—so much that could have happened, and so much that did. It ended with Swann catching a rocket from Bradshaw that traveled at least 70 yards in the air, Swann jumping and taking it on the Dallas five-yard line and gliding in for the touchdown, and Bradshaw barely conscious on the ground after being decked by the Cowboys' Cliff Harris on a safety blitz....

As for Bradshaw, he could only try to recall what reality was like. "I got hit right here," he said, pointing to his left cheek. "They were coming. I could feel them coming. I don't know how I got the ball off. I was hearing bells or something on the ground...."

"Was it exciting?" Cowboys tight end Jean Fugett said. "I guess it was. I guess maybe we can't play a dull game."

Neither can Lynn Swann. And the combination of Dallas's being there and Swann's rising to the occasion—up, up and away—made it something for everybody in Miami to take home to think about until next year. Who said the Super Bowl is dull?

kansas city **Chiefs 23**

minnesota **Vikings 7**

The conversation may or may not have been taped. After calling to wish the Kansas City Chiefs good luck before Super Bowl IV, President Richard Nixon told Chiefs head coach Hank Stram to pass a message to his quarterback, Len Dawson. The message was this: Tell Len not to worry about the gambling allegations.

"I don't know that it constituted a Presidential pardon," Stram later said, "but it sure made Leonard feel better."

More so than any quarterback in Super Bowl history, Dawson felt pressure to play an error-free game. Five days earlier, NBC's "Huntley-Brinkley Report" led with news that a Justice Department task force investigating gambling was on the verge of compelling seven pro football players "to testify on their relationship with known gamblers." Dawson's name was on the list.

He would be exonerated later, and indeed had already been cleared by the NFL, after an exhaustive investigation—a fact which did not prevent Dawson

from having The Week From Hell. Besieged by media scrutiny, he slept poorly, and on the eve of the game literally worried himself sick.

Oddsmakers predicted a hellish Sunday for him, too. At Tulane Stadium in New Orleans, Dawson would be trying to move the ball against the Minnesota Vikings and those alliterative cannibals of renown, the Purple People Eaters, otherwise known as the Minnesota front four. Vegas liked the Vikes by two touchdowns.

To spend any time at all with Stram in the days before the game was to be convinced that those odds were skewed. The Chief's voluble coach saw this game as nothing less than a showdown between football's past and future. Whereas the Vikings were a team of the '60s— "the decade of simplicity," said Stram—his mod squad belonged to the future. He pointed to KC's newfangled IHOP defense, the "triple-stack," and 18 offensive formations as evidence of his own cutting-edge credentials.

Nor did it hurt that in placekicker Jan Stenerud and punter Jerrel Wilson, Stram had arguably the best kicking game in Super Bowl history. Stenerud set the tone for the day with a 48-yard field goal on Kansas City's first possession. Two more field goals and a five-yard touchdown run by Mike Garrett—he scored easily, on a trap play to which the Purple People Eaters were susceptible—gave the AFL

In the face of intense media scrutiny, Dawson (left) had a brilliant game, completing 70 percent of his passes and avenging Kansas City's Super Bowl I defeat.

Bill Brown (30) and the the Vikings sputtered against the Chiefs' triple-stack, gaining just 67 yards rushing.

representative a 16–0 halftime lead.

On defense, the triple-stack was flummoxing Minnesota. Thinking their All-Pro center Mick Tingelhoff could handle Kansas City middle linebacker Willie Lanier, the Vikings expected to run at the middle. To keep Tingelhoff off Lanier, Chiefs defensive tackles Buck Buchanan and Curley Culp lined up on the center's head and worked him over all afternoon. The Vikings didn't rush for a first down until the third quarter.

The triple-stack defense was not insoluble—Minnesota merely played as if it was. It didn't work if the opponent ran to the weak side. "But they never varied from their game plan," Chiefs defensive end Jerry Mays would say. "They kept running into our strength." The Vikings made no major halftime adjustments. Said their stoic head coach, Bud Grant, "Just play better." No Minnesota player is on record as replying, *Just coach better.*

In handing the NFL its second straight Super Bowl loss, Dawson completed 12 of 17 passes for 142 yards and a touchdown. Those num-

bers reflect his mastery of a vaunted Vikings defense, and—considering his personal travails that week—a remarkable fortitude and focus.

When it was over, Dawson accepted the telephoned congratulations of a certain football-crazy chief executive—didn't Nixon have a country to run?—and the MVP award. Such plaudits meant little next to his restored reputation. Afterward, Dawson spoke of a "tremendous burden being lifted." He stopped talking at one point, then grinned and said, simply, "I'm vindicated."

postgame

The Minnesota Vikings had no way of knowing it at the time, but being the second straight NFL team to lose the Super Bowl to the upstarts from the AFL was the least of their worries following Supe IV. Their 23–7 loss to the Chiefs began a run of Super Bowl defeats that would saddle the Vikings with a choker reputation they have yet to shake.

Still, the Vikings, with Hall of Fame quarterback Fran Tarkenton and the Purple People Eater front four of Alan Page, Jim Marshall, Gary Larsen and Carl Eller, were among the best teams of the '70s. They returned to the Super Bowl after the '73 season only to meet the defending champion Miami Dolphins, who won 24–7. Out went one powerhouse opponent, in came another: The Pittsburgh Steelers downed the Vikes 16–6 in Super Bowl IX. Two years later Minnesota returned to the Big Game to face the Oakland Raiders. The Raiders had lost six AFL or AFC title games since 1968. The winner of this game would shed the loser label for good. Alas, the Raiders romped 32–14 and went on to win Super Bowls XV and XVIII. Minnesota still stands at 0–4 in football's biggest game.

The strong right foot of Stenerud accounted for 11 of the Chiefs' 23 points on two extra points and three field goals, including this 48-yard boot in the first quarter.

pittsburgh **Steelers 35**
dallas **Cowboys 31**

What was this man doing on the defensive? As the Pittsburgh Steelers' quarterback, Terry Bradshaw should have commanded a certain amount of deference in January 1979: He had already won two Super Bowls and as many games as any quarterback in history. But there he was in the week leading up to Super Bowl XIII, scrambling for his dignity and answering questions about his IQ and his toupée.

In those days, Bradshaw's Louisiana twang and zany sense of humor led many to the conclusion that he was a bit simple. Dallas linebacker Thomas (Hollywood) Henderson did not exactly repair this misperception when he told reporters in Miami—in the most repeated quote of the Super fortnight—that Bradshaw "couldn't spell cat if you spotted him the 'c' and the 'a.'"

So it came to pass that the 30-year-old future Hall of Famer found himself defending his intelligence and his decision to wear a

hairpiece. "When I put on my wig, I feel young," said Bradshaw, whose hair had thinned since he quarterbacked the Steelers to a narrow victory over the Cowboys in Super Bowl X. His ability to make good decisions in a game and his poise in the pocket, meanwhile, had expanded along with his pate. Dallas would get a much-improved Bradshaw this time around.

While the defenses had been dominant in Supe X, this game would be more of a quarterback's duel. Other plotlines required no updating. Cowboys safety Cliff Harris again tried in vain, as he had three years before, to rattle Steelers wide receiver Lynn Swann. This time, all Swann did was catch seven passes for 124 yards and score the game-winning touchdown.

Pittsburgh was still about brawn—"We're gonna kick their ass, put it in the bank," Steelers defensive tackle Mean Joe Greene had growled the day before the game—and Dallas was still about deception. A botched reverse on the Cowboys' fifth play from scrimmage set up an early Pittsburgh touchdown, after which the Steelers promptly surrendered two. A pair of Bradshaw TD passes, one a 75-yarder to John Stallworth and the other an improvised, 7-yard toss to Rocky Bleier, made it 21–14 at the half.

Both Bradshaw and Dallas quarterback Roger

**Anchoring a more pass-oriented offense this time around,
Bradshaw stood tall and threw for 318 yards and four touchdowns.**

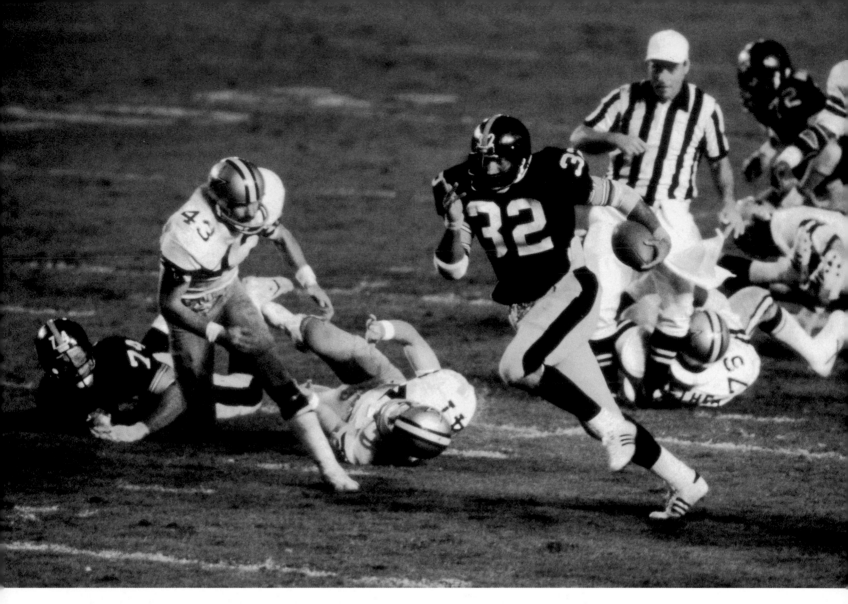

DAN JENKINS (1/29/79)

For Pittsburgh, nobody dropped anything that mattered. Stallworth's two touchdown plays were very different, and they both say something about Bradshaw. The first was a cunning 28-yard beauty—the Steelers call it "One Eleven Out"—that Bradshaw thought would take advantage of [Aaron] Kyle on Stallworth, man-for-man, and it did. Stallworth got behind Kyle and caught the ball easily in the end zone.

The second came at what might be described as a mildly opportune time: in the second quarter, after the Cowboys had taken their 14–7 lead by virtue of the Brink's job that Henderson and [Mike] Hegman had performed on Bradshaw. Bad shoulder or no bad shoulder, Bradshaw was right back running for his life again. This time he found Stallworth at the Pittsburgh 35. Stallworth fought off a glancing blow by Kyle—more or less a flesh wound—and, using a couple of blocks and his speed, outran everybody for the score.

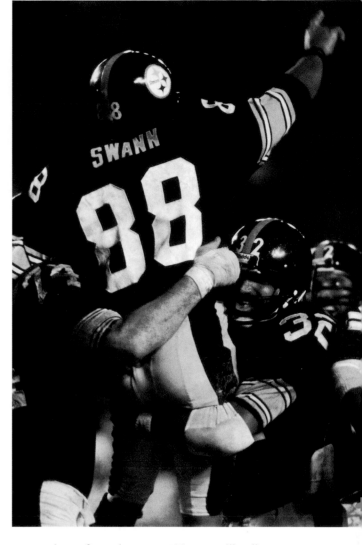

While Harris (opposite, top) found daylight and Swann (right) claimed the end zone, a wide-open Smith (opposite, bottom) earned nothing but ignominy after dropping a potential game-tying pass from Staubach in the third quarter.

Staubach would complete 17 of 30 passes. Staubach threw for 228 yards and three touchdowns; Bradshaw passed for 318 yards and four TDs—both Super Bowl records. Of course, Roger the Dodger would have had a fourth TD pass in the books if 38-year-old tight end Jackie Smith, whom Dallas coach Tom Landry had talked out of retirement before the season, had caught that third-quarter lollipop pass in the end zone instead of letting it bounce off his shoulder pads. If Smith catches the gimme, the Cowboys pull even, 21–21.

In Smith, Cowboys fans found a tragic victim. In field judge Fred Swearingen they found a despised villain. Swann and Cowboys cornerback Benny Barnes became entangled running under a Bradshaw rainbow in the fourth quarter.

"He tripped me," said Swann.

"He pushed me," said Barnes.

Swearingen flagged Barnes for pass interference.

In the moments that followed, the Cowboys lost the Super Bowl. Four plays after what some Texans still call the Phantom Interference, Franco Harris scored on a trap play from 22 yards out. Dallas defensive tackle Randy White fumbled the ensuing kickoff and Dennis (Dirt) Winston recovered for the Steelers. Bradshaw found Swann in the back of the end zone on the very next snap.

After the game, Henderson stopped weeping long enough to say, "I rated [Bradshaw's] intelligence, not his ability." Bradshaw, for his part, was beyond caring. "I don't need anyone telling me how great or how smart I am, or how smart I'm not," he said. He had a third, gaudy ring. And he wasn't done yet.

pittsburgh **Steelers 31**
los angeles **Rams 19**

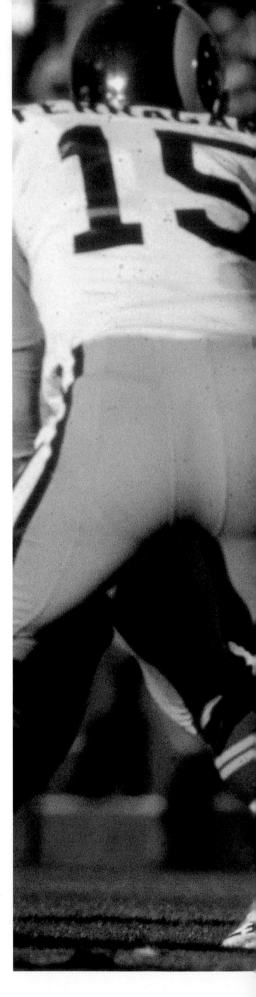

They were booed by their own fans, regularly and with gusto. Prior to their unlikely march through the playoffs, the rabble-in-arms Los Angeles Rams had dropped five of their final 11 regular-season games. They finished the year 9–7. Now, with an offense that hadn't scored a touchdown in the NFC title game, an offense led by a quarterback making his eighth NFL start, the Rams would try their luck against mighty Pittsburgh and the Steel Curtain defense. One NFL general manager had said of the Pittsburgh D, "Don't send the Marines to Iran. Send the Steelers."

The prospect of winning a fourth Vince Lombardi Trophy in six years inspired Steelers defensive tackle Mean Joe Greene to refer to the game as "an invitation engraved in gold." An invitation to what? "To immortality," he said.

While the Steelers played like a team under the impression that victory would be theirs if they simply showed up at the Rose Bowl,

gilded invites in hand, Vince Ferragamo drove the Rams to scores on two of their first three possessions. As it became clear that Ferragamo was not crippled by the jitters, Rams head coach Ray Malavasi, oft criticized for his uninspired calls, cast his inhibitions to the Santa Ana winds. Fourth-and-eight on the Steelers 37? Go for it! The Rams did, with Ferragamo hitting the immortal Billy Waddy with a hard strike for the first down. The play set up a field goal that gave the Rams a 13–10 lead at halftime.

The Steelers answered on their first possession of the second half as Lynn Swann made a leaping 47-yard touchdown catch to add yet another bit of brilliance to his Super Bowl resume. The Rams responded with sleight-of-hand. A 24-yard halfback option pass from Lawrence McCutcheon to Ron Smith gulled Pittsburgh corner Ron Johnson and put the Rams back on top, 19–17.

If the Steelers had been sleepwalking, as was rather forcefully suggested to them by middle linebacker Jack Lambert—"He hollered so hard in the huddle, I got scared," recalled strong safety Donnie Shell—the whistle at the end of the third quarter served as a wake-up call. Chief among the somnambulants had been quarterback Terry Bradshaw, who'd fought insomnia by night and inaccurate passing by day in the week leading up to the game.

Lambert turned his trademark menace on his own teammates and they responded by shutting out the Rams in the final period.

Until Greene (75) and the Steel Curtain shut him down in the fourth quarter, Ferragamo played a solid game.

Through three quarters of Super Bowl XIV, he had thrown three interceptions. Early in the fourth quarter, however, on third-and-eight from Pittsburgh's 27, the balding Louisianan finally achieved wakefulness.

The call was 60 Prevent Slot Hook and Go, and Bradshaw didn't like it. Pittsburgh had run it eight times in practice that week without completing it once. This time, though, wideout John Stallworth sold Rams cornerback Rod Perry on an inside move, caught the pass and outran strong safety Dave Elmendorf for a 73-yard game-winning touchdown. Stallworth gained 45 yards on the same play two series later to set up an insurance TD.

MVP voters ignored Bradshaw's interceptions and obeyed the unwritten rule: When in doubt, give the award to the winning quarterback. So in addition to a fourth Super Bowl ring, Bradshaw picked up that extra accolade, even though his center, Mike Webster, observed, "Ferragamo was the better quarterback today."

In the end, the courage of the upstart Rams could not top the sheer talent of the dynastic Steelers. "God-given ability," said Webster, one of seven future Hall of Famers on that legendary Pittsburgh team. "You just can't beat it."

postgame

Following the Rams' surprisingly close game against the heavily favored Pittsburgh Steelers in Super Bowl XIV, Los Angeles quarterback Vince Ferragamo sat in front of his locker and told reporters, "We're young. We'll be back."

With that utterance he violated a fundamental maxim of professional sports: Most players finish their careers without a title shot, so don't take your opportunities lightly. And it came back to haunt him. Not that Ferragamo didn't make the most of his Super Bowl. Some called him a better quarterback than Terry Bradshaw that day. But his cavalier assumption that the Rams would reach that rarefied air again proved unfounded. After an 11–5 season in 1980 (and a first-round playoff loss), Ferragamo left the NFL for the Canadian Football League. The Rams dropped to 6–10 in 1981. Ferragamo was back in '83 and led the team to the second round of the playoffs, but the Rams would not approach the Super Bowl again until '85, when they lost 24–0 to Chicago in the NFC title game. By that time, Ferragamo was with 2–14 Buffalo. He retired the following year.

The Steelers took over in the fourth quarter after a 73-yard Bradshaw bomb settled into Stallworth's hands.

san francisco **49ers 26**

cincinnati **Bengals 21**

This was the start of something big, the San Francisco 49ers' first Super Bowl appearance. There was already talk from a few brave souls that the Niners might be the team of the '80s. There was just one problem: 95 minutes before the kickoff for Super Bowl XVI, half of The Team Of The Decade was missing.

Bus No. 1 had arrived at the Silverdome in Pontiac, Mich., on schedule. Bus No. 2, which left the team's hotel 15 minutes after Bus No. 1, was mired in a traffic jam caused by the motorcade of Vice President George Bush, who probably lost some votes in the Bay Area that day. Bill Walsh, in his third season as San Francisco's head coach, did not react the way a typical NFL head coach would have. "Coach Walsh was pretty loose on the bus," quarterback Joe Montana reported later. "He said, 'I've got the radio on and we're leading 7–0. The trainer's calling the plays.'"

The country was still finding out about Walsh. The aquiline features and silver hair, so familiar now, had yet to become icons of football excellence. No one yet knew how dangerous this guy could be with an extra week to prepare.

Very dangerous, it turned out. While Cincinnati had been judged to be the more talented team, Walsh kept them off balance the entire game, with, among other things, a bit of razzle-dazzle dubbed the Short Yardage Triple Pass. This play was a Rube Goldbergesque flea-flicker in which no fewer than four 49ers handled the ball. Fretting about his offense's ability to make short yardage, Walsh installed an unbalanced line formation the day before the game.

"Happens all the time," said Montana. "We were afraid we were going to get a new play on our way to the game."

Walsh's predilection for new wrinkles extended to special teams: Having noticed how the ball tended to skid on the Silverdome's unforgiving, seven-year-old AstroTurf, he had his kicker, Ray Wersching—who would make four field goals in four attempts in the game—work on a newfangled kickoff called the hard squib. The Bengals made no significant runbacks of the squirting, unpredictable kick, and their return man, two-time Heisman Trophy winner Archie Griffin,

The 49ers' scrappy goal-line stand in the third quarter allowed San Francisco to maintain its 13-point lead and keep the surging Bengals at bay.

PAUL ZIMMERMAN (2/01/82)

Here are some of the new plays the San Francisco 49ers put in but did not use against the Cincinnati Bengals: an end-around pass; ... a pitch-and-lateral, quarterback Joe Montana to running back Ricky Patton to tight end Earl Cooper; something called a nickel blizzard, which is a safety blitz out of the nickel-back formation. What else? Oh, yeah, "short-yardage triple pass," ... no, wait a minute, the Niners did use that. They used it in the first half, when they were building a 20–0 lead....

Maxims of the playoffs: You dance with who brung ya; you don't get away from your strength; people win, not formations. Forget them, says Walsh, the mind in motion, a walking collection of X's and O's seeking only a blackboard, a piece of lined paper, a napkin, anything. The triple pass, in which Montana hands to Patton, who hands to wide receiver Freddie Solomon, who pitches back to Montana, who throws to tight end Charle Young, was designed for third-and-one. It made its entry on the Niners' first third-and-one situation, picked up a neat 14 yards and then bowed out for the day.

The world soon learned what Walsh could do with an extra week.

fumbled one squib. That turnover set up the field goal that gave the Niners a 20–0 halftime lead.

But Cincinnati would not fold. After quarterback Kenny Anderson scored on a five-yard run to make it 20–7, the Bengals were poised to score again with a first-and-goal on San Francisco's three-yard-line. On first and second downs, they ran Pete Johnson up the gut; twice the 250-pound fullback failed to score. On one of those thrusts, 49ers inside linebacker Jack (Hacksaw) Reynolds made the hit of the game, stymying Johnson and nearly knocking himself out in the process. On third-and-goal at the one, San Francisco linebacker Dan Bunz ranged outside to wrap up Charles Alexander on a swing pass. No gain. Fourth down: Johnson was repelled again. The Bengals had eaten

nearly six minutes of clock and come away with nothing to show for it.

The Niners threw two passes the rest of the way, and Wersching kicked his third and fourth field goals. Cincinnati quarterback Ken Anderson, having run for one score, threw for two more, but it was not enough.

No sooner had the 49ers hoisted the Lombardi Trophy than they found themselves answering questions about whether or not they would dominate the decade. Reporters, it seemed, had moved on to the next storyline. Surely the Niners just wanted to enjoy the moment, but with 27 players 25 years old or younger on their roster, five of them fresh draft picks, and Walsh minding the controls, they must have known the best was yet to come.

After the game, the football in Montana's hands was replaced with the Lombardi and MVP trophies.

the teams

The Teams

The fat man was on the ground, gasping and pleading. It was July 10, 1989, the first day of Jimmy Johnson's second minicamp. The Dallas Cowboys' first-year head coach had his players submit to a modest workout: sixteen 110-yard sprints in 100-degree heat. Now, one particularly gelatinous lineman was on the grass, saying, "Coach, I got asthma!"

"Asthma my ass! This isn't the asthma field," shouted Johnson, who had the offending player removed from his sight, and, not long after, from the roster. In his first year as head coach of the Miami Dolphins in 1996, Johnson opened a midseason press conference by saying "This is nothing personal against [starting free safety] Gene Atkins, but we have released him." Atkins had been burned for the game-winning touchdown the day before.

If Jimmy tended to go about tearing down his teams

The legendary Lombardi (near right) built a 1-10-1 team into an NFL champion a mere three seasons later.

with untoward zeal, it was because he so looked forward to building them back up.

It is an ineluctable element of drama, and, it seems,
of truly great NFL teams: Before you ascend the
mountain, you do some time in the valley. In 1958,
Packers head coach Ray (Scooter) McLean scooted
out of Green Bay, bequeathing a 1-10-1 team to new
coach Vince Lombardi. Two years later that team
played for the NFL championship. Veteran members
of the Pittsburgh Steelers laughed out loud in 1969

when, in his first speech to his new team, coach
Chuck Noll declared that it was his goal to win the
Super Bowl. The Steelers roared out of the gate, winning their opening game 16–13 over Detroit. They
then lost the next 13.

Four stupendous drafts and five years later, Pittsburgh
stood astride the league like a colossus. Its final Super
Bowl season coincided with the arrival in San Francisco
of coach Bill Walsh, who was always uncomfortable
being called the Genius. But no one was calling him Fin-

The 1979 season ended with Chuck Noll's Steelers, led by the indomitable Terry Bradshaw (left), winning their fourth and final Super Bowl, 31–19 over the Los Angeles Rams; it also marked the debut of Walsh (right), who would need three seasons to establish himself as the NFL's resident genius.

stein in '79, when his Niners went 2–14. It was not until three seasons later, when San Francisco won the first of its five Super Bowls, that Walsh was awarded his Mensa membership by popular acclaim.

Critics of Johnson had a field day during the '89 season, when the Cowboys lost 15 of 16. Johnson repelled the brickbats with his industrial-strength 'do, however, and his Cowboys won a Super Bowl three years later.

Each of these men who presided over NFL dynasties got the very best out of his players. Whether it was Lombardi molding into champions essentially the same players who had performed so miserably under a different coach, or Noll, Walsh and Johnson drafting the kind of players that would fit into their well-devised schemes, these coaches had the undiluted respect of their players and got them to produce their best when it mattered most: on Super

Sunday. No mean feat, that. Consider Buffalo Bills coach Marv Levy. A sure bet for the Hall of Fame, Levy took the Bills to four straight Super Bowls. Yet the Bills do not make our list of the Top Ten Super Bowl teams in NFL history because they lost all four. Clearly they were a dominant team. Why couldn't they win the big one? Were they unprepared, mentally or tactically? Unlucky? Not good enough? Probably a bit of all of the above, for as all winning Super Bowl coaches will attest, everything has to come together for your team on that momentous Sunday if you are to hoist the trophy named after the first coach to win the Big Game, Lombardi.

And it's not getting any easier. In this era of salary caps and big-money free-agency, the entropic forces dismantling great teams are stronger than ever. Let this serve as a beacon of hope for the NFL's have-nots—all you Cardinals, you Seahawks, you Falcons, you Saints remember: Even the best teams toiled for long years in the valley before ascending the mountain.

s a n   f r a n c i s c o **49ers**

mountaintop

Beauty and perfection do not necessarily make for good TV. In fact, only 39% of American households tuned in to San Francisco's 55–10 whitewashing of Denver in Super Bowl XXIV, the lowest Supe rating since 1969. But those who did witnessed a 49ers team that could play every kind of football with surgical precision. San Francisco's first possession set the tone: 66 yards in 10 plays capped by a 20-yard TD pass from Joe Montana to Jerry Rice. On the first TD drive of the second quarter, nursing a 13–3 lead built largely on passing, Montana dished off to running backs Roger Craig and Tom Rathman on 13 of 14 plays. With the clock running out in the first half, Montana, who had been hammering the Broncos with short stuff, went 38 yards to Rice for the second of Rice's three TDs on the day. In all, Montana connected with seven different 49ers and threw for a Super Bowl–record five touchdowns on 22 for 29 passing. In an era of alleged parity, the 49ers trounced their three playoff opponents by a cumulative score of 126–26. When rookie coach George Siefert said of a possible three-peat, "If they want to do it again, that's fine with me," TV execs must have winced.

The empire-building had been going on for years. It is nonetheless possible to pinpoint the day—indeed, the play—that marked the dawning of the Age of the San Francisco 49ers. On Jan. 10, 1982, with 58 seconds left in the NFC title game, the Niners had the ball on the Dallas six-yard line, trailing the Cowboys 27–21. Joe Montana called Sprint Right Option—one of his options being, when all else failed, to chuck the ball out of the end zone. That may or may not—accounts differ—have been what Montana was trying to do when, hemmed against the right sideline by Dallas defenders, he let it fly.

Dwight Clark had no way of knowing either, as he gathered himself to jump, whether he was pursuing a ball intended to be uncatchable. With Cowboys cornerback Everson Walls a step behind, reduced to the role of dread-filled spectator, Clark made the leap of his life, snagging Montana's throwaway at the apex of his jump, with the tips of his fingers. It was not just a hell of a catch, it was The Catch, and it did not just win the game, it expunged one of the NFL's homelier legacies: Prior to the arrival of head coach Bill Walsh in 1979, this team had not won an NFL championship or Super Bowl in its 29 years as an NFL franchise. Over the next 14 years, the 49ers would go to five Super Bowls and win all five, an unmatched record in the Big One.

A fortnight after The Catch, The City By The Bay went bananas after its team held off the Bengals to win Super Bowl XVI. One reveler told an AP reporter, "Now San Francisco is No. 1 in two things—being weird and football."

To say nothing of weird football. After inheriting a team that had gone 2–14 in '78, Walsh phased in his West Coast offense, an iconoclastic, cart-before-the-horse system which used the pass to set up the run. While Walsh did not disdain big plays, he didn't waste downs trying to make them, either. He preferred to subject defenses to prolonged ordeals. Said Walsh, "The goal is to attack the other side with sharp, clean blows while you're moving faster than the opposition. That was von Clausewitz."

People didn't call this guy The Genius for nothing. Walsh was not just another head coach with an unread copy of Sun Tzu's *The Art of War* on his desk. He was as comfortable dropping ref-erences to the Prussian military strategist Carl von Clausewitz as he was discussing playwright Robert Ardrey or ethnologist Konrad Lorenz. The man had range. In addition to being the finest football strategist of his generation, he had an eye for talent.

In Super Bowl XXIII, Montana engineered The Drive that beat the Bengals (again). Having secured his third Super Bowl victory in eight seasons, Walsh retired, but the groundwork he had laid yielded two more championships under head coach George Seifert.

While the 1986 draft engineered by Walsh was perhaps the most productive in Niner history—the team netted fullback Tom Rathman, wideout John Taylor, defensive end Charles Haley, tackle Steve Wallace and corners Don Griffin and Tim McKyer—it was not atypical of the franchise. San Francisco's ability to retool on the fly kept its dominance alive and brought Super Bowl victories following the 1989 and '94 seasons. Roger Craig gave way to Ricky Watters, more self-centered but equally talented. Clark retired and was replaced by Jerry Rice, the best ever to play his position. Montana grudgingly ceded the reins to Steve Young, who threw for a record six touchdowns in Super Bowl XXIX, a 49–26 gutting of the San Diego Chargers.

No matter how many new faces don 49ers red-and-gold, however, Clark will never be forgotten. The team's fortunes turned on his Catch. After that first Super Bowl win over the Bengals, San Franciscans rioted in the streets. Dozens of people were hospitalized. "I hope it's another 35 years before they win another championship," groused one policeman.

No such luck, pal.

Montana, no mere mortal in the regular season, was truly superhuman in his four Super Bowls, racking up 1,142 yards, 11 TDs and no interceptions.

<h1>dallas **Cowboys**</h1>

Smith and Aikman led the resurgent Cowboys to three Super Bowl titles in four seasons in the '90s.

in SI's words

PAUL ZIMMERMAN (1/02/89)

[Prior to Super Bowl VI, Duane Thomas] had gone through his famous Silent Season. He had stopped talking—to the media, the coaches, most of his teammates, everyone. So here we were on Super Bowl Monday … 20 writers ringing Thomas and witnessing his silence. This eeriest of all Super Bowl interviews lasted maybe 20 minutes.

I close my eyes now and see Thomas, slashing and swerving for 95 yards behind a line that executed its cutoff and trap blocks with military precision.

In the press box, an editor for *Sport,* the magazine that gives the Most Valuable Player award—a car—had polled us for our choice. It was practically unanimous for Thomas.... When the winner was announced as Roger Staubach, who had rather moderate stats (12 of 19 passes for 119 yards), we let out a groan.

The award is a promotional thing, and I still don't understand why the NFL doesn't step in and take it over. The car is given at a ceremony, and the recipient is expected to say a few words. I figure that let Thomas out.

The Dallas Cowboys sprinkled the 1970s with five Super Bowl appearances, dolloped the '90s with three. Their eight appearances are unmatched—no other franchise has more than five—and with their five Super Bowl wins they tie San Francisco for the most alltime. In the bellbottom era, the Cowboys made it to the Big Game with Aristotelian regularity: at the beginning, middle and end of the decade. If not for a last-second field goal by the Baltimore Colts in '71 they might have come out with a winning record in those five. As it happened, they won two (VI and XII) and lost three (V, X and XIII). But make no mistake, this was a dominant team. These were the Cowboys of Roger Staubach and Bob Lilly, the Doomsday Defense and the only coach the franchise had ever known, Tom Landry. They won seven division titles and went to the playoffs nine times in the '70s.

Naturally, then, it was considered heresy by the Dallas faithful when Jerry Jones unceremoniously sacked Landry immediately after purchasing the team in February 1989. But the game had passed Landry and the once proud Cowboys by. They'd gone 3–13 in '88. The new owner brought in his own coach, Jimmy Johnson, thereby replacing the man in the fedora with a coach whose ossified coiffure alone practically qualified as a hat. And the mousse-abusing Johnson soon had a controversy of his own to handle. In hindsight, it wasn't so much a controversy as it was a charade. In the supplemental draft in July '89, the Dallas Cowboys selected ex-Miami Hurricane quarterback Steve Walsh, even though they'd taken a quarterback in that spring's regular draft—a guy named Aikman.

"I really think it's going to be a coin flip," predicted third-string quarterback Babe Laufenberg. "I get the call if the coin lands on its edge."

Was it a genuine competition? "Absolutely," replied Johnson, straightfaced. Did Walsh really have a shot at unseating Troy Aikman? Probably not. Traded in '90 to the New Orleans Saints, Walsh went on to an unremarkable career while Aikman quarterbacked the Cowboys to those three Super Bowls in the '90s, all victories.

Talk of a Super Bowl for the '89 Cowboys was farfetched and ridiculous: The sad-sack Pokes lost all but one of their games. Johnson made 46 trades in his first four seasons, none so audacious, and, it turned out, lopsided, as the blockbuster he swung during the '89 season, when he dealt running back Herschel Walker to the Minnesota Vikings for a king's ransom of five veteran players and eight draft picks. Dallas's rebuilding had begun in earnest. The Cowboys' drafts from '89 to '93 yielded 15 starters. The offensive stars Jones refers to as the Triplets—wideout Michael Irvin, Aikman and running back Emmitt Smith—were the Cowboys' first-round picks in '88, '89 and '90, respectively.

Dallas's ascent was steep and swift and culminated in its return to the Super Bowl in January '93. In what was their NFL-record sixth appearance in the Big One—but their first in 14 years—the Cowboys forced nine turnovers and annihilated the Buffalo Bills 52–17. The game's only drama involved the Cowboys' quest to break the record for most points scored in a Super Bowl. They would have done it if Leon Lett had not held the ball out like a waiter bearing a tray of hors-d'oeuvres as he neared the goal line on a long fumble return in the fourth quarter. In the game's most memorable play, Bills receiver Don Beebe slapped the ball out of Lett's hands, and the Cowboys settled for a 35-point victory.

In Super Bowl XXVIII the following season, Dallas beat Buffalo again, 30–13. Two months later, after a clash of egos between Johnson and Jones resulted in Johnson's resignation, the self-described bootlegger's boy, non-sequitur-spouting Barry Switzer, took over as Dallas's coach. Although the Cowboys won Super Bowl XXX under Switzer, it was widely believed that the team succeeded in spite of, rather than because of, its head coach. The Cowboys' 1997–98 season began with Switzer attempting (inadvertently, he insisted) to carry a firearm onto a flight and ended with him resigning under pressure after a 6–10 season.

As the '98 season approached, the Cowboys dynasty appeared to have gone belly up. But one could not be too sure. The Triplets, after all, were still on board.

p i t t s b u r g h **Steelers**

Why would a promising young coach climb aboard this train wreck of a franchise? In 1969 Joe Paterno decided there was no good reason to do so, and told Pittsburgh Steelers owner Art Rooney to find someone else to be his new head coach. So Rooney, who had purchased the team 36 years earlier with winnings from a good day at the track, settled on his second choice, a gimlet-eyed Baltimore Colts defensive backs coach named Chuck Noll, whose stern visage concealed an active intellect. As a messenger guard for Paul Brown's Cleveland Browns, Noll had spent three seasons attending law school at night. During his tenure as Steelers head coach, it was a well-kept secret that Noll seldom missed a concert by the Pittsburgh Symphony, and that he enjoyed puttering among the geraniums in his greenhouse.

Finding and cultivating talent was another Noll specialty. Pittsburgh's draft harvests from '69 through '74 yielded seven future Hall of Famers and stocked arguably the most fearsome dynasty the game has ever seen. Noll's Steelers won four Super Bowls in six years, and the '76 team that didn't make it to the Big Game might have been the best of them all.

The hot rookie in '72 was Franco Harris, whose Immaculate Reception in the playoffs against the Oakland Raiders that season was the watershed for the franchise. Pittsburgh trailed the Raiders 7–6 in the game's final seconds when quarterback Terry Bradshaw rifled a desperation pass in the direction of running back Frenchy Fuqua, who was leveled by Oakland safety Jack Tatum, off whom the ball caromed ... into the hands of Harris, who raced down the left sideline to deliver the Steelers their first-ever playoff victory. Two seasons later they would win their first of four Super Bowls.

In 1974, Noll presided over the greatest spring haul in NFL history. In the first five rounds of that year's draft, the Steelers selected linebacker Jack Lambert, center Mike Webster, and wide receivers Lynn Swann and John Stallworth. The Steelers beat Minnesota 16–6 the following January in Super Bowl IX, with MVP Harris outrushing the Vikings 158 yards to 17.

The Steelers were just warming up. "Our best team ever was '75," said defensive tackle Mean Joe Greene. "We knew from day one where we were going." They were going to Super Bowl X in Miami, where Swann would literally and figuratively rise above

---

The Steel Curtain, led by Lambert (58) and Greene (75), powered Pittsburgh to back-to-back Super Bowl wins in the '70s.

---

in SI's words

PETER KING (01/13/92)

Chuck Noll seldom gave a good interview in this media-driven age. He never gave his players pats on their backs, which drove some, most notably Terry Bradshaw, bananas. He was slow to change with the game, acting as his own special-teams coach until 1987. But when he resigned on Dec. 26, 1991, he left the biggest void atop a team since Vince Lombardi retired from the Packers in '68. In Noll's 23 seasons as Pittsburgh's coach, his steely, steady hands guided the team to 12 playoff appearances and four Super Bowl victories.

"Chuck never fell into the twin pitfalls of ego and greed," New York Giants general manager George Young said. "He always had his life and his role in football in perspective. He cared more about the teaching of football than listening to accolades and selling himself in commercials." Noll never hawked a product. All he wanted to do was coach . . . that and be invisible.

Noll's legacy? There's a clue in something he said in a recent interview. "Don't leave anything on the beach but your footprints," he said. You figure it out.

the Dallas Cowboys, who had sought to intimidate him in the wake of his recent concussion. Swann made four acrobatic catches for 161 yards and one touchdown in a 21–17 win.

Even though the Steelers were idle on the following Super Sunday—missing Harris and his running mate, Rocky Bleier, due to injuries, they'd lost to the revenge-minded Raiders in the AFC championship—they fielded what may have been the best defense in NFL history. Powered by future Hall of Famers Lambert, Greene, linebacker Jack Ham and defensive back Mel Blount, Pittsburgh allowed zero TDs in eight of its final nine games, and pitched three straight shutouts. This was the Steel Curtain at its steeliest.

It was all a bit much for the NFL Competition Committee. Before the '78 season, that august group—chaired by Dallas Cowboys president Tex Schramm—decreed that defensive contact with receivers five yards beyond the line of scrimmage would be illegal. The new stricture came to be known as "the Mel Blount rule" and the Steelers, who had a decent quarterback and some pretty fair receivers themselves, made it work for them. Bradshaw led the AFC in passing that season and threw four touchdown passes in Super Bowl XIII as Pittsburgh held off the Cowboys, 35–31. Nice try, Tex.

In a game whose final whistle tolled the death knell of the dynasty, the Steelers beat the Rams, 31–19, in Super Bowl XIV. That Pittsburgh failed to win "one for the thumb"; that as of 1998 it has been back to the Super Bowl just once without winning, cannot diminish the stature of those '70s Steelers: They were a team for the ages.

green bay **Packers**

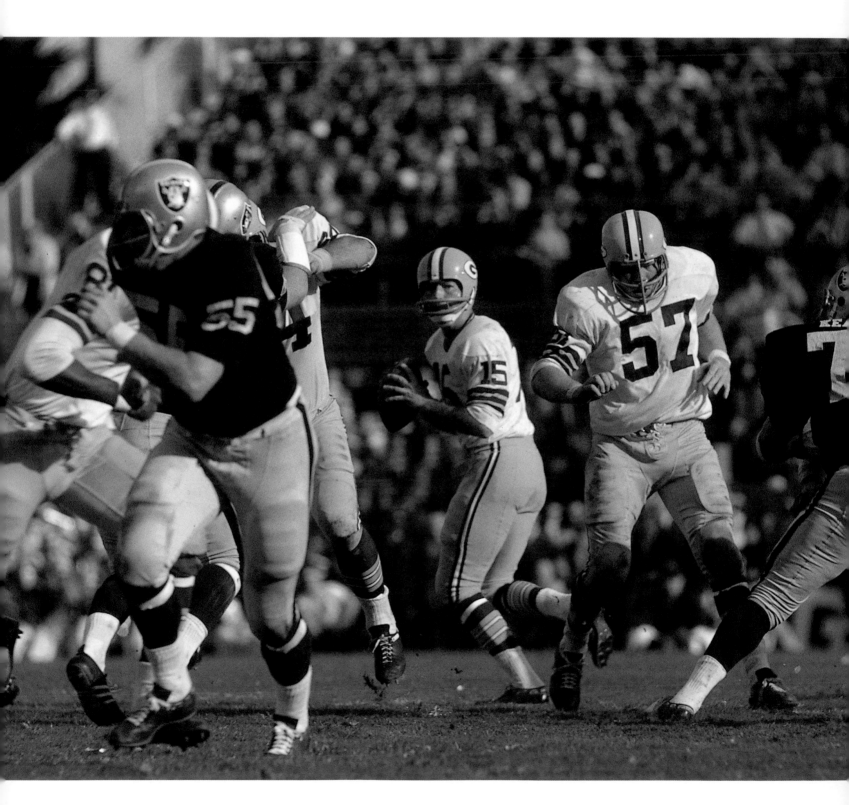

in SI's words

RON FIMRITE (1/27/86)

It may well be true that Lombardi's methods, his preachiness, his fanatical devotion to the work ethic would not win him this sort of unflagging loyalty from today's far wealthier and certainly more independent athletes. But the Packers of Super Bowl I were scarcely robots....

Their common bond was Lombardi, actually the love of Lombardi. Some years after Lombardi's death in 1970, [Jerry] Kramer asked [Herb] Adderley if he thought often of his old coach. "Every day," Adderley replied. "And I love my father, who is also deceased, but I don't think about my father every day...."

Lombardi's great team would also win Super Bowl II, beating the Oakland Raiders 33–14. And then, sadly, it would all be over. In 1969 Lombardi would leave Green Bay for the Washington Redskins, and a year later he would be dead.... All of their lives went in different directions, some down, most up, but they never lost that sense of community that made them so strong in their playing days. Their time as athletes has passed, but what a time it was.

Football genius though Vince Lombardi may have been, his public relations instincts left something to be desired. Lombardi's plan for the inaugural Super Bowl, to be played in the Los Angeles Memorial Coliseum in 1967, was to show up in L.A. just before the kickoff. That way his players could be spared the ravages of the southern California heat, not to mention other regional distractions to which notorious Packers carousers such as running back Paul Hornung and receiver Max McGee might be susceptible.

No dice, said NFL commissioner Pete Rozelle. You'll spend the week out here, promoting the game. So Lombardi and his squad holed up in Santa Barbara, 90 miles north of L.A., where he growled at his players during practices, "We're not here to look at the mountains!"

Lombardi had to be a micromanaging despot to get his team out of the cellar. A year before his 1959 arrival, Green Bay had a win and a tie in 12 games. The Packers had stunk for so long that the NFL was considering dropping them. Along came this bespectacled oracle to the football gods, who told his underachieving charges—including Hornung, fullback Jim Taylor, quarterback Bart Starr, tight end Ron Kramer, guard Jerry Kramer, lineman Forrest Gregg and center Jim Ringo—"You will make mistakes, but not very many if you want to play for the Green Bay Packers."

Three years later, the Pack won the first of five NFL titles it would win over the next seven years. Its fourth NFL crown came in 1966 and, for the first time, did not signal the end of the season. The first Super Bowl would follow, though at the time it wasn't called the Super Bowl; the tickets for the game read AFL-NFL WORLD CHAMPIONSHIP GAME.

Green Bay's opponent, the Kansas City Chiefs, felt rightly that they had nothing to lose; as representatives of the nascent AFL, they could hardly be expected to knock off the mighty Packers. Cornerback Fred Williamson personified the Chiefs' come-what-may attitude. Williamson was known for his patented "Hammer," a forearm chop to the helmet, which he promised to drop on Green Bay's receivers. The Packers may not have feared the Hammer, but they feared sullying the NFL's reputation by losing. They were tight as kickoff approached.

Starr's Packers, facing the Chiefs and the Raiders (left) in the first two Super Bowls, upheld the honor of the senior circuit against the upstart AFL.

None of them was quite so tight as McGee had been the night before while barhopping in L.A. McGee rolled into his hotel room shortly after dawn on game day, and was not at all pleased when starting receiver Boyd Dowler separated his shoulder on the Packers' first offensive series. Nevertheless, McGee trotted out and caught a 37-yard touchdown pass to put the Pack up, 7–0. Starr had thrown the ball behind him, but the 34-year-old McGee reached back and caught it one-handed, as nonchalantly as a man snagging a tossed bottle of Old Milwaukee.

To the dismay of fans of the senior circuit, Green Bay could not shed the Chiefs, and led by the surprisingly slim margin of 14–10 at halftime. That was as good as it got for K.C., though, as the Pack turned up the heat in the second half and won, 35–10. In the fourth quarter, Williamson was knocked unconscious on a running play. As he was carried off the field on a stretcher, Packers guard Fuzzy Thurston could be heard humming the tune "If I Had a Hammer".

After Green Bay's 33–14 hammering of Oakland in Super Bowl II, Lombardi retired as the Packers' coach, and Green Bay enjoyed all of five winning seasons over the next 24 years. In '92, the Packers traded for a raw, 22-year-old quarterback named Brett Favre. Right away, the losing seasons stopped, and the Pack returned to the Super Bowl in 1997, defeating New England 35–21.

Only an inspired performance by the Denver Broncos the following January kept Green Bay from another run of back-to-back titles. But by winning the first two Super Bowls and appearing in two straight to close the 1990s, the Packers had bookended the Big Game in this century with their excellence.

washington **Redskins**

For a decade they were at or near the top. The Washington Redskins appeared in four Super Bowls between 1983 and '92, winning three of them, with three different starting quarterbacks.

While personnel and strategies came and went, the common denominator in D.C. during the Redskins' golden decade was a humble, bespectacled head coach who unfailingly thanked God after victories and whose saltiest exhortation, according to Redskins free safety Mark Murphy, was "Let's kick their buns!"

When Joe Gibbs was brought in to replace Jack Pardee in 1981 the Redskins had not won a championship of any kind since 1942. After an 0–5 start that had the nation's capital feeling nostalgic for Pardee, Gibbs's team righted itself and finished at .500. As the surging Skins headed into the playoffs the following season, running back John Riggins told Gibbs he needed more work. "I need the ball," said the man known as The Big Diesel. "You got it," replied Gibbs.

Thus did Riggo invite his teammates to climb on his back and ride through the postseason. He carried the ball 25, 37 and 36 times, respectively, in Washington's three playoff wins leading up to their confrontation with the Miami Dolphins in Super Bowl XVII. Then, with a title on the line, Riggins rushed 38 times for 166 yards against a Dolphin D ostensibly designed to shut him down, keying a 27–17 Redskins win.

"Ron's the president," said MVP Riggins after the game, referring to the occupant of 1600 Pennsylvania Avenue. "But I'm the king."

Dethroned a year later by the Los Angeles Raiders, the Redskins returned to the NFL title game after the '87 season. During that year Gibbs called backup quarterback Doug Williams into his office to tell him he'd been traded to the Raiders. Six hours later, Gibbs changed his mind. "I can't do it," he told Williams. "I feel, somewhere along the line, you're going to win this thing for me."

Fast forward to Super Bowl XXII, in which Washington faced the Denver Broncos. After beating out Jay Schroeder for the quarterback job during the season, then losing the job due to an injury, then winning it again, Williams ended his rollercoaster season on a high. A nosebleed high. He became, in rapid succession, the first black quarterback to start in a Super Bowl, and the first quarterback, period, to throw four touchdown passes in one Super Bowl quarter.

Alvin Garrett's touchdown in Super Bowl XVII provoked this celebration from the group of Washington running backs and receivers known as the Fun Bunch.

surprise star

While it may not have seemed surprising at the time, Mark Rypien's MVP performance in Super Bowl XXVI certainly catches one's eye in hindsight. Rypien is easily the most low-profile quarterback ever to lead his team to victory in the Super Bowl. Among the flashy Namaths, Montanas and Bradshaws, he stands out like a beige leisure suit. A sixth-round draft pick out of Washington State in 1986, Rypien hit his stride in coach Joe Gibbs's system during the '91 season. He threw for 3,564 yards, had a 97.9 passer rating and led the Skins to a league-best 14–2 record. When he passed for 292 yards and two touchdowns in the Redskins' 37–24 romp over Buffalo in Supe XXVI, it was impressive but not all that surprising given the season he'd just had. The following season, however, Rypien threw four more interceptions than touchdown passes. In '93 his passer rating plummeted to 56.3 and the year after that he was shipped to Cleveland, where he appeared in six games. He has not had a starting job since and has bounced from Cleveland to St. Louis to Philadelphia and back to St. Louis.

His Super Bowl XXVI performance looks more surprising with each passing year.

But even his triumph had a rollercoaster beginning: Denver quarterback John Elway staked his team to an early 10–0 lead, while Williams hyperextended his left knee. Williams returned in the second quarter and, "Before we knew it," said Elway, "they had 35 points."

"Let's get this sucker rolling," said Williams when he entered the huddle. And off it went. Ricky Sanders sold Broncos corner Mark Haynes on a hitch-and-go: Williams hit him for an 80-yard score. Walking to the sideline after that play, Washington's massive lineman Joe Jacoby told Williams, "White, black, green, yellow—you're our quarterback."

Williams threw for three more touchdowns before halftime (rookie Timmy Smith rushed for a 58-yard score during the quarter), and the Redskins, who went conservative in the second half, won 42–10. The second-quarter outburst was the most remarkable one-quarter offensive display in NFL playoff history.

Said Williams, "Sixty points wasn't out of reach." He began the season as a backup and finished it as MVP of the Super Bowl. But the rollercoaster did not stop there. Williams started just 12 games over the next two seasons, and hit the waiver wire in 1990. *Sic transit gloria*. When the Redskins returned to Super Bowl XXVI in '92, it was Mark Rypien who quarterbacked them to a 37–24 win over the Buffalo Bills.

A year later, Gibbs retired. With a television career beckoning, he walked away from the game, but not without having kicked some serious bun.

l . a . / o a k l a n d **Raiders**

So many years have gone by since this team has won a playoff game that it is possible to forget that, long ago, back when the Vegas-lounge-singer wardrobe of owner Al Davis was only a decade or so behind the fashion curve, his "Raiduhs" actually intimidated other teams. For the first 20 years of Super Bowl competition, the Silver and Black played in the AFC or AFL title game 11 times. From 1977 to '84, the Raiders made it to three Super Bowls and won them all.

They were on their way in '72 until the Immaculate Reception, the famous catch by Pittsburgh Steelers running back Franco Harris, who snared the ball inches from the turf after it had ricocheted off two players, and ran for the winning touchdown as time ran out in the Raiders' first-round playoff game. Oakland avenged this crushing loss in the '76 AFC title game, thumping Pittsburgh 24–7. "We hate them, they hate us," said Raiders quarterback Kenny (The Snake) Stabler afterward. "Beating them that bad was sweet indeed." But not as sweet as Oakland's 32–14 win over the Vikings in Super Bowl XI that season, after which, the Snake fondly recalled, "Freddie [Biletnikoff] was crying and Coach [John] Madden was all red and grinning and guys were hugging each other like a bunch of fruits."

But there was little love between Stabler and Davis, the Raiders' owner. Oakland lost in the AFC title game the following season, and failed to make the playoffs in '78. "If you've got to find someone to blame," Davis said, "blame Stabler." By the time the Raiders made it back to the Super Bowl following the '80 season, Stabler had been replaced at quarterback by Davis-reclamation-project Jim Plunkett, who during a Super Bowl–week press conference was asked: "Let me get this straight, Jim. Your mother is blind and your father is dead. Or is it the other way around?"

Unfazed by callous queries and the Philadelphia Eagles pass-rush alike, Plunkett threw three touchdown passes in Oakland's 27–10 triumph. That win gave the Raiders their second Super Bowl victory and the week leading up to it firmly established, on a national stage, the franchise's reputation as the NFL's halfway house.

With players blowing off practices and ignoring curfews—6'8",

---

A season after being cut by the 49ers, Plunkett threw a trio of touchdown passes to lead the Raiders to victory in Super Bowl XV.

mountaintop

Few Super Bowl teams have had as fitful and arduous a climb to greatness as the Raiders. They ascended the mountain repeatedly during the 1960s and '70s, only to be repelled just shy of the summit each time. After losing to the Green Bay Packers 33–14 in Super Bowl II, the Raiders made it to six of the next eight AFL or AFC title games, and lost all six.

They finally broke the jinx in the 1976 AFC championship game, knocking off the two-time defending champion Pittsburgh Steelers 24–7 to advance to Super Bowl XI. Their opponents, the Minnesota Vikings, had a similar history of Big Game disappointments, having come up short in Super Bowls IV, VIII and IX. Their respective histories notwithstanding, one of the losers had to win.

The outcome was never really in doubt. Led by Clarence Davis's slashing running (16 rushes for 137 yards) and Kenny Stabler's pinpoint darts (12-of-19 passing for 180 yards), the Raiders overcame an early blocked punt and cruised to an easy 32–14 victory. With that first Super Bowl title finally under their collective belt, the Raiders went on to win two more in the '80s.

280-pound defensive tackle John Matuszak was chief among the curfew breakers—the Raiders accumulated in the neighborhood of $15,000 in fines during Super Bowl week. Philadelphia coach Dick Vermeil tut-tutted that if Matuszak were an Eagle, "he'd be on his way home before the game."

The Tooz, for his part, thought the Eagles lost because their coach was too uptight. Davis agreed, saying, "It's tough to have a paramilitary group within the confines of a culture that isn't paramilitary."

Similarly, it's tough to maintain order in a league when its owners pick up and leave on a whim. Ignoring the express wishes of the NFL and an eminent domain suit filed by the city of Oakland, Davis pulled up stakes after the '81 season and relocated his team to Los Angeles. In its second season in southern California, the franchise claimed its third Super Bowl in a 38–9 whipping of the Washington Redskins. The game's MVP was Marcus Allen—a local boy allegedly drafted by Davis to boost attendance at the L.A. Coliseum—who rushed for 191 yards, including a spectacular 74-yard touchdown run on the last play of the third quarter.

Allen and Davis would part ways under a cloud in 1992, and Davis would move his peripatetic team back to Oakland in 1995. Over the next four seasons the iconoclastic head man would fire three coaches and watch his team lose more games than it won. Every so often though—as in a '97 victory over that year's eventual champion Denver Broncos—the team would show flashes of its vintage form. Those flashes were a reminder that, back in the glory days, the Raiders slogan was The Pride And The Poise.

m i a m i **Dolphins**

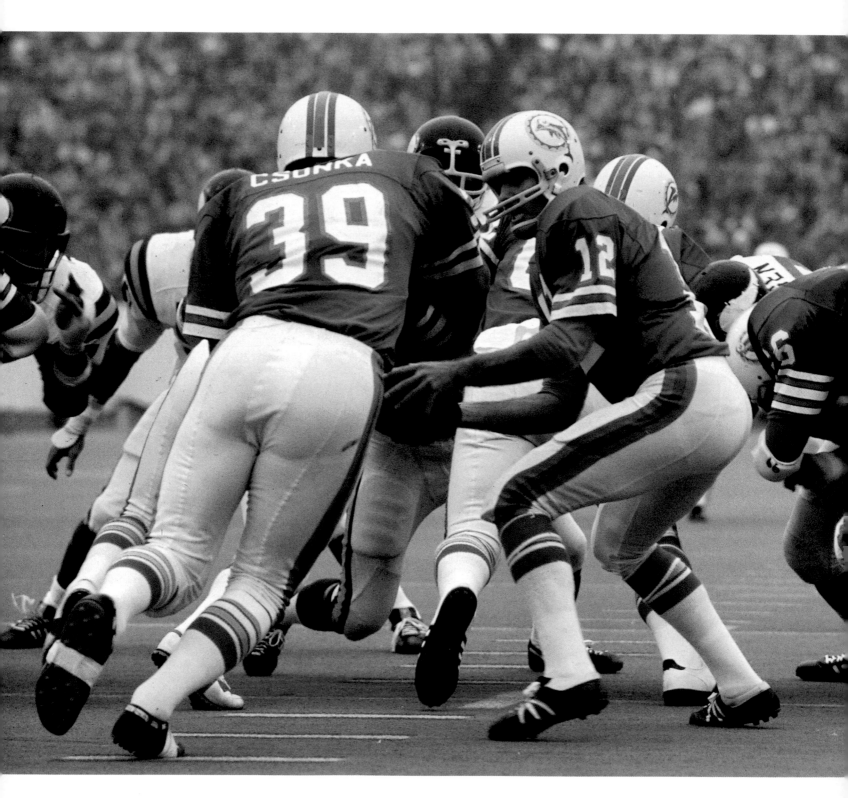

Flush from victory in Super Bowl XXXI and eager to believe media accounts of their team's potential for dominance, a handful of Green Bay Packers predicted before the 1997 season that completing the schedule undefeated was not an unreasonable goal for them.

Memo to NFL players: Next time you feel the need to make like Kreskin and foresee an undefeated season for your team, lie down until the urge passes. To make it through a season with a goose egg in the loss column requires equal and prodigious portions of talent and luck. The feat has been accomplished but once in NFL history, by the '72 Miami Dolphins, whose 14–7 defeat of the Washington Redskins in Super Bowl VII was their 17th victory against zero defeats.

Despite losing two games the following season, the '73 Dolphins were actually a better team than the undefeated '72 edition, winning emphatically when it mattered. In Super Bowl VIII they beat the Minnesota Vikings—the Buffalo Bills of the '70s—by 17 points.

Other teams have boasted more talented rosters; other teams have won more championships. But give these guys their due: For two seasons, this Dolphins team was one for the ages. Miami's 32–2 record over those two seasons is an NFL record, as was its appearance in three straight Super Bowls until the Bills surpassed it with four straight appearances (all losses) in the Big Game from '91 to '94. Prior to their perfect season, the Fish had flopped in Super Bowl VI, losing 24–3 to the Dallas Cowboys, whose coach, Tom Landry, unwittingly coined a nickname when he claimed he didn't know the names of any of Miami's defensive players.

The No-Name defense held Miami's first five opponents of 1972 to an average of 13 points. In Game 6, the Dolphins beat the Buffalo Bills, 24–23, with a 54-yard field goal by Garo Yepremian, a diminutive, balding Cypriot whose strong kicking leg was not complemented by an equally strong throwing arm, as the nation would later discover. "I remember later reading our yearbook about the unbeaten season," Yepremian said, "and thinking, *my god, what if I didn't make the 54-yarder?*"

Posing a greater threat to Miami's historic season was a Week 5 injury to quarterback Bob Griese, who suffered a fracture of his

---

Csonka (39) and the Dolphins enjoyed a perfect 1972 season and suffered only two regular-season losses en route to Super Bowl VIII the following year.

surprise star

Led by linebacker Nick Buoniconti, free safety Jake Scott and tackle Manny Fernandez, the Dolphins' No-Name Defense had a different standout every game. In Supe VII it was Scott, the first defensive back ever to earn Super Bowl MVP honors. (He was finally joined by Larry Brown in 1996.) With just over five minutes left, the Dolphins in front 14–0 and Washington at the Miami 10, Scott picked off a Billy Kilmer pass in the end zone and ran it back 55 yards. It was his second interception of the day and it put an emphatic end to a Washington drive that had covered 79 yards, the team's longest of the game. During Miami's return trip to the Super Bowl against Minnesota the following year, Scott recovered a fumble off a Buoniconti tackle at the Miami one to stop a critical Viking drive late in the first half. The play spelled the end of Minnesota's title chances. Two years later, after racking up 35 interceptions in six seasons with Miami, the five-time Pro-Bowl safety asked to be traded. His relationship with Coach Don Shula, once a father figure of sorts, had visibly cooled. Scott played three seasons, ironically enough, with the Redskins, before being cut in 1978 and retreating to his remote Colorado cattle ranch.

right fibula and a dislocation of his right ankle in a 24–10 win over the San Diego Chargers. Onto the field lumbered 38-year-old, crew-cut, waiver-wire pickup Earl Morrall, who led the team all the way to the Super Bowl, at which time head coach Don Shula returned the reins of the offense to the recovered Griese.

The success of the Morrall's interregnum was largely due to Miami's record-breaking rushing game. Running through holes opened by the likes of All-Pro guard Bob Kuechenberg and future Hall of Famers center Jim Langer and tackle Larry Little, Larry Csonka and Mercury Morris both rushed for over 1,000 yards. The Dolphins' 2,960 rushing yards were an NFL record. Yet it was the iconoclastic running back Jim Kiick, whom Morris had supplanted as starter during the regular season, who scored three important postseason touchdowns, including the game-winning score against the Redskins in the Super Bowl, a dull contest in which Washington did not cross midfield until late in the first half. The Skins' sole touchdown came on an interception return in the fourth quarter, but the passer responsible was neither Griese nor Morrall. It was Yepremian, who made a slapstick attempt to pass the ball after his 42-yard field-goal attempt was blocked.

Miami won a second straight Super Bowl, only to see its dynasty prematurely snuffed out by the emergence of the World Football League, a short-lived rival circuit which lured away Csonka, Kiick and receiver Paul Warfield. It was eight years before Miami won another playoff game.

It will be much, much longer before another team achieves what the '72 Dolphins did: perfection.

n e w   y o r k **Giants**

surprise star

The Giants' magic 1990 season seemed in danger of running off the rails. After a 10–0 start, the team had lost three of four games, and in the last of those defeats, a 17–13 decision to the Buffalo Bills, quarterback Phil Simms went down with a severely sprained right foot. The Giants had already clinched a playoff berth, but with an offense led by backup Jeff Hostetler, who had only two NFL starts under his belt, it was uncertain how far they could go in the postseason.

But Hoss calmly took the reins and closed out the regular season with two victories. In the first two rounds of the playoffs, against Chicago and San Francisco, he completed 25 of 44 passes for 288 yards, two touchdowns and no interceptions; he also rushed for 43 yards and a score against the Bears.

On Super Sunday against the Bills, Hostetler completed 20 of 32 passes for 222 yards, and led New York on a Super Bowl–record 9:29 scoring drive in the third quarter, completing three clutch third-down passes along the way. Hostetler's heroics gave the Giants their second Super Bowl title, and when Simms returned, a contentious quarterback controversy.

When the time comes for the people at the Hall of Fame in Canton, Ohio, to decide what they want to etch on Bill Parcells's plaque, they will likely omit reference to a decision he made at the start of the 1983 season, his first as head coach of the New York Giants. That's when the Tuna—the nickname that adhered to Parcells in the early '90s—benched quarterback Phil Simms and handed the reins to the immortal Scott Brunner.

"It was a mistake, okay?" Parcells said years later. "I was a new coach. I hadn't seen that much of Phil. The other guy had taken us to the playoffs. What can I say?"

Being Parcells means never having to say you're sorry. Before retiring from football after the '90 season (he would later unretire, coach the New England Patriots to a Super Bowl, then return to New York as apparent savior of the woeful Jets) the Tuna brought Gotham a pair of NFL titles. It didn't hurt that he eventually changed his mind and went with Simms. After setting Giants records for passing in '84 and '85, the first-round draft pick out of Morehead State turned in one of the most nerveless performances in Super Bowl history. With the entire nation wondering how John Elway would fare against the formidable New York defense in Super Bowl XXI, Simms stole the spotlight from his more famous counterpart, completing 22 of 25 passes in a 39–20 Giants romp.

The Broncos had led 10–9 at halftime, but while Simms led the Giants offense to four touchdowns and a field goal in its first five possessions of the second half, the Giants defense held the Broncos to two yards of total offense. Game over. The previous spring at the NFL draft in New York, Parcells and Giants general manager George Young had used six high picks on defensive players—even though New York already had a notoriously gnarly D featuring Lawrence Taylor, Harry Carson, Leonard Marshall and Carl Banks, the linebacker who spearheaded the Giants' spirited goal-line stand in the second quarter.

It should be noted, too, that two of New York's three scores in that historic quarter came off trick plays. A fake punt kept a drive alive, leading to the first touchdown, and a Simms-to-Joe Morris-to-Simms-to-Phil McConkey flea-flicker went for 44 yards and set up the third score. One of Parcells's great assets was his

---

The New York defense, led by Taylor, turned Super Bowl XXI into a rout after a late first-half sack of Elway produced a safety that reenergized the team.

ability to adhere to his abiding principles—control the ball on offense, stuff the run on defense—while avoiding predictability. With Denver's linebackers, in the Tuna's words, "all gassed up" to get after running back Morris, Parcells kept them on their heels by having Simms throw a variety of play-action passes. The Giants passed on nine first-down plays in the first half. In the second half, having convinced the Broncos to think pass, the Giants broke out the battering ram.

"They changed their whole offensive attack," said Broncos linebacker Karl Mecklenburg. "Pass first, run second. It surprised us. We thought they would try to establish the running game, but they went against their tendencies, and they did a good job of it."

The Tuna was truer to his conservative tenets in Super Bowl XXV, a game that presented a stark contrast in styles: the no-huddle, hi-tech Buffalo Bills versus the wide-body, low-tech Giants. With the league's oldest starting running back, 34-year-old Ottis Anderson, running behind a mammoth line, the Giants held onto the ball for more than two thirds of the game. When Buffalo did have it, the Giants' defensive backs funneled Bills receivers inside, to the neighborhood of Banks and Pepper Johnson, who took their lunch money and knocked the spit out of them. After Buffalo kicker Scott Norwood's famous 47-yard field goal miss assured the Lombardian Giants of their second Lombardi trophy in four years, Parcells was seen in the winners' dressing room repeating the same sentence like a mantra, which, to him, it was: "Power wins football games."

chicago **Bears**

After turning his head into a billboard, getting acupuncture in his buttocks and mooning a helicopter, Chicago Bears quarterback Jim McMahon went out and played a fine game in Super Bowl XX, scoring on a couple of sneaks and throwing for 256 yards. Despite his herculean efforts to dominate the spotlight before the game, McMahon will be remembered as an oddment, a supporting player to the men who decided this 46–10 rout of the overmatched New England Patriots.

Meet the Junkyard Dogs: Mike Singletary, Wilber Marshall, Richard Dent, Dan Hampton, Steve McMichael, Otis Wilson and the rest of a ravening Bears defense which came into this game having shut out its previous two playoff opponents. For an encore, it staged the most dominant performance by any unit, offensive or defensive, in Super Bowl history.

Even when the Patriots caught a break, they ended up giving aid and comfort to the the enemy. After New England recovered running back Walter Payton's fumble on the game's second play, quarterback Tony Eason threw three straight incompletions, pumping up the Dogs. The Pats got a field goal out of it, but their offense would scarcely be heard from the rest of the way.

Next Patriots series: two more incomplete passes and a 10-yard sack of Eason. Only one of New England's first 10 offensive plays, in fact, went for positive yardage—a three-yard rush by Craig James. Despairing of running on Chicago's notorious "46" defense, Patriots head coach Raymond Berry had hoped to catch the Bears off guard by throwing. Passing, however, requires pass-blocking, and the Patriots, who yielded seven sacks, couldn't accomplish the second part of the deal. Right guard Ron Wooten likened his team's attempts to protect its quarterbacks to "trying to beat back the tide with a broom."

The Patriots finished the first half with minus-19 yards of total offense, and the game had been all but decided, essentially, after two series. With 5:08 left in the second quarter, Berry pulled the shellshocked Eason, replacing him with Steve Grogan, who engineered New England's sole touchdown, an extraneous, fourth-quarter score.

Shortly after the game Bears defensive coordinator Buddy Ryan would announce that he had accepted the Philadelphia Eagles head

---

With Singletary (50) directing traffic, the Dogs ran wild, registering seven sacks, forcing four fumbles and holding the Pats to a meager 0.6 yards per rush.

in SI's words

CURRY KIRKPATRICK (2/03/86)

Chicago coach Mike Ditka admitted that the McMahon phenomenon took the "pressure" off the rest of the Bears and was something "relatively sane. Now if Jim went out and robbed a McDonald's or something, that would be insanity." This is the same coach who complimented McMahon for possessing "the guts of a burglar" after the quarterback scored two TD's in that 46–10 dog and pony show that passed for a championship game on Sunday.

Before McMahon enlivened that dreary proceeding, even Pete Rozelle had confessed that the NFL was getting a kick out of McMahon. That should have told you something. Among other things, the commissioner called our boy "a fascinating folk hero"— obviously in direct retaliation for a Boston radio-talk-show host's denigration of McMahon as a "carefully programmed phony flake."

It took 20 years but finally the ultimate cult showman had emerged in the sporting world's ultimate pop-art event. All McMahon did was play hard, have fun, win and force football fans everywhere to look deeper into this bloated activity that has become the Super Bowl and chuckle at it, him and themselves.

coaching job. The imminence of his departure caused the curmudgeonly coordinator to grow misty-eyed during a defensive team meeting the night before the game. "Win or lose, you guys are my heroes," he said as tears ran down his face. "We gave him a standing ovation," recalled defensive back Dave Duerson. "Then McMichael threw a chair at the chalkboard."

In the game's waning minutes, Bears defenders surrounded team president Mike McCaskey, pleading with him to retain Ryan. "If we lose Buddy Ryan we'll be a good defensive unit, but if we keep him," promised Hampton, "we'll be in the Super Bowl the next five years."

The Bears lost Ryan and, over the next three years, due to free agency and retirement, six of the starters who had given Chicago its first title in any major professional sport since 1963. Asked to describe his feelings after the game, Payton deferred, saying, "It won't really sink in till next year. Right after we win it again." You couldn't fault his confidence, given the talent that surrounded him in the locker room that day.

The fact that as of 1998 the Bears have not been back to the Big Game cannot detract from their dominance that Sunday afternoon in New Orleans in 1986. Chicago was unbeatable, its defense utterly dominant. After that early Patriots field goal, a message on the scoreboard noted that 15 of the 19 teams to score first in previous Super Bowls had won the game. Mike Singletary saw that message.

"I thought, yeah, but none of those 15 had ever played the Bears."

denver **Broncos**

Despite the fact that the team did not enjoy a winning record until 1973, its 14th season in existence, the Denver Broncos have sold out every game at Mile High Stadium since 1970. To call Broncos fans long-suffering doesn't quite capture their condition; their suffering has been barbed by hopes cruelly raised, then callously crushed.

The pattern began in 1977, when Denver rang up a 12–2 record and won the AFC West. On Christmas Eve that season, in its first-ever playoff game, Denver's Orange Crush defense, led by end Lyle Alzado and linebacker Randy Gradishar, outplayed the Steel Curtain, and the Broncos beat Pittsburgh 34–21. But three weeks later in Super Bowl XII the Broncos fell on their collective face, turning the ball over eight times in a 27–10 loss to the Dallas Cowboys.

A precedent had been set and would be adhered to long thereafter: A terrific regular season generates Mile-High hopes, only to end in not just disappointment, but also embarrassment and humiliation.

The Broncos returned to the Super Bowl after the '86 season thanks to the wizardry of fourth-year quarterback John Elway. In the final minutes of regulation in the AFC title game against the Cleveland Browns, Elway submitted the first chapter to his storied career, driving Denver 98 yards for the game-tying touchdown in the closing moments of regulation (a Rich Karlis chip shot won it in OT, 23–20). The Drive, as the sequence would thereafter be known, yielded to The Disaster of Denver's second half against the New York Giants in Super Bowl XXI. For two quarters, Elway matched Phil Simms completion for completion. In the second half, Simms earned the MVP award while Elway learned that, to win one of these Roman numeral games, it helps to have a little help from your defense.

Another pattern emerged in Denver's postseason travails. Like the guy who kicks his dog before going to work to get yelled at by his boss, the Broncos regularly abused the Browns in the AFC title game before submitting to their inevitable, ritual humiliation at the hands of their Super Bowl opponent. With Cleveland on the verge of scoring the tying touchdown in the '87 AFC championship game, reserve cornerback Jeremiah Castille ripped the ball from

---

After three fruitless trips to the Super Bowl, Elway (7), blessed at last with a capable supporting cast, emerged with a win in his fourth.

in SI's words

PAUL ZIMMERMAN (1/02/89)

The final score [at Super Bowl XII in 1978] read Dallas 27, Denver 10, but this is how close it really was: Early first quarter, scoreless game, the Superdome going crazy, Tony Hill fumbles a Denver punt on his own one. The ball's bouncing, and Denver's Randy Rich and Ron Egloff are diving for it. So is Hill. And he gets there first. Dallas's ball.

I am convinced that if the Broncos had recovered that fumble and punched it in for a score, they would have won. Their defense was ready for mayhem—that great Orange Crush unit had all the Denver fans wacky. On the Cowboys' opening play they sent Butch Johnson in motion and ran him on an end around. Check Tom Landry's record in Super Bowls: He usually likes to start off with some sort of flimflammery. The Broncos swarmed the play. Tommy Jackson, a linebacker, spilled it for a nine-yard loss. With that kind of inspiration, fortified by a 7–0 lead, I figure the Bronco defense would have risen up and taken the Cowboys apart....

The problem was that I hadn't thought it through. I forgot that Craig Morton and the Denver offense had to get out there and do their bit too. Going into the AFC Championship Game against the Raiders, Morton had barely been able to walk.

---

running back Earnest Byner's grasp and recovered the fumble, allowing Denver to cling to victory ... and making possible the Broncos' 42–10 annihilation by the Redskins in Super Bowl XXII.

To rev up his team for their playoff run after the '89 season, Denver coach Dan Reeves placed two of the Broncos' three Lamar Hunt trophies—symbolizing the team's AFC titles won under Reeves—in a team meeting room. The players were underwhelmed. Said Elway, "I need one of those big ones with the football on top."

Elway got the Broncos another chance to do just that by turning in the best game of his career to date—a three-touchdown, 385-yard passing effort in the AFC title game against, of course, the Browns. Asked to make a prediction going into Super Bowl XXIV against the San Francisco 49ers, Reeves did not project tremendous confidence when he answered, "We'll show up."

Elway was the last guy out of the Broncos dressing room after Denver's 55–10 defeat. Asked by wide receiver Michael Young if he was okay, No. 7 shook his head. "They'll never, ever forgive me for this," he said, referring to the Broncos' long-suffering fans.

The arrival in 1995 of an unheralded running back named Terrell Davis allowed Elway, in the twilight of his career, to get some redemption. While Elway performed merely adequately in Denver's fifth Super Bowl appearance, Davis was superb, rushing for 157 yards and three touchdowns against the Green Bay Packers. And the Broncos, at long last, took home one of those trophies with the football on top.

HALFTIME:

T h e   S c e n e

Of course, no look at the Super Bowl would be complete without an examination of the hoopla that surrounds this bold, garish, quintessentially American event. Herewith a collection of snapshots taken away from the action, a Super Sampler if you will, designed to showcase the Big Game and its attendant hubub. Welcome to the Super Spectacle.

56   FINAL INSTRUCTION

:04   INTRODUCTION (OFFENSE)

:09   COIN TOSS

5:13   K.O/RET ON RESPECTIVE
       35 yd LINE, FACING FAR-end.

5:13:30 Moment of Silence — Hubert
         Humphry — MARTin Luther King.

5:14   NATL AnThem

As important as a coach's pregame speech—such as the one delivered by Green Bay's Mike Holmgren above—might be, many players will always take the route of Desmond Howard (below) who sought his inspiration from a higher source.

Since 1967, when the Kansas City Chiefs trotted onto the field for Super Bowl I (left), the big game has only gotten bigger, attracting increasingly massive television audiences and turning Super Sunday into an unofficial national holiday; in 1978, the detailed pregame plan (above) called for a moment of silence in memory of Martin Luther King's birthday and the death of Hubert Humphrey.

Frenzied fans: Some like *Tonight Show* regular Doc Severinsen (left) and the Bengal afficionados at far left trumpet their adulation, while others such as the Redskin faithful below simply try to hog the spotlight.

#4 + #92 = 1

Go Pack!

BROWN

13

Behold the power of Cheese™

Behold the power of Cheese

OFFICIAL CHEESEBUTT CUSHION

Something about the Super Bowl causes otherwise mild-mannered spectators such as the Denver fan above to go doggone overboard, though few can match the sheer cheesiness of the Green Bay boosters (right).

Beloved Pittsburgh owner Art Rooney (near left) waited 42 years before Franco Harris (far left) and the '70s Steelers enabled him to light a victory cigar for an NFL championship.

Key architects of the matchup originally known as the "World Championship Game" included (above, left to right) Kansas City coach Hank Stram, NFL commissioner Pete Rozelle and Chiefs owner Lamar Hunt; on Super Bowl Sunday, Joe Montana (left) often faced his toughest blitz not on the field but from the media following the game.

Fanfare extraordinaire: From the Rockettes in 1988 (above) to the rockets' red glare in '96 (right) to the New Orleans jazz band in '90 (below), the Super Bowl has always been about more than just football.

Just how big has the Super Bowl become? In 1993, the halftime show featured the gloved one himself, Michael Jackson (below).

The halftime showboating (above in 1990) has often been more spectacular than the game itself; in '93 the nation's most renowned cheering section, the Dallas Cowgirls (left), got a chance to strut their stuff on football's biggest stage; unfortunately for the Raiders in Super Bowl II, the Packers seemed almost as large on the field as they were in symbolic form off it (right).

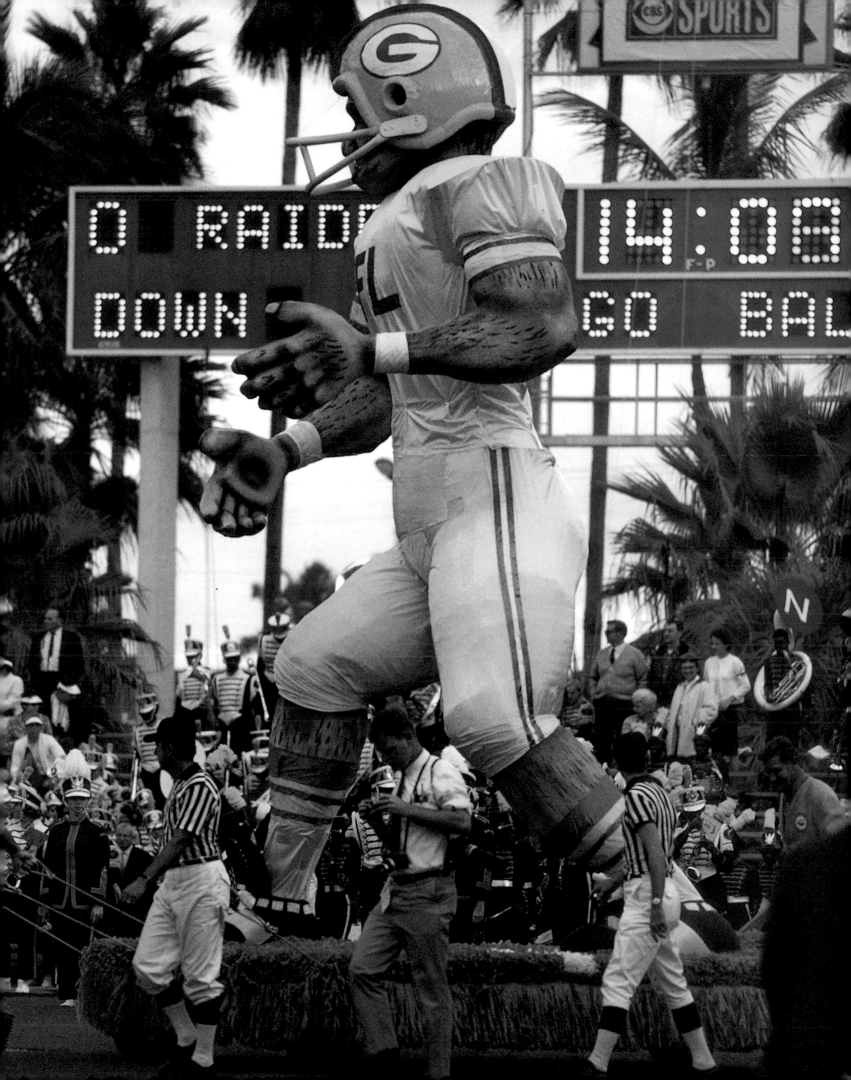

Both Sides Now: While Denver's Bill Romanowski (right) and New York's Everson Walls (above) embodied the joy of victory, Dallas's Cliff Waters (above right) and Green Bay's Mark Chmura (far right) viewed the Super Bowl through losers' eyes; the Giants showered Bill Parcells (left) with affection—and Gatorade—after they beat the Broncos in Super Bowl XXI.

the players

The Players

The subject was San Francisco quarterback Joe Montana. The speaker was venerable Dallas Cowboys president Tex Schramm, who observed, "In history, there seem to be great people who come around at a certain time. He was one of those."

The tortured syntax and general vagueness of the passage notwithstanding, we think we know what ol' Tex was talking about. Greatness has a lot to do with timing.

But great timing is not the only thing these 20-odd Super heroes have in common. They went into their respective Big Games with a steely confidence, an imperviousness to pressure that enabled them to excel on one of the world's largest stages. Either that, or they got really lucky. How else to explain Green Bay

wide receiver Max McGee playing out of his gourd in Supe I with a Titanic-sized hangover?

Some overcame tremendous odds to reach the peak of their profession. Once-waived, once-traded quarterback Jim Plunkett was plucked from the scrap heap by the Raiders, whom he led to two Super Bowl wins. The MVP of Supe XX, Chicago Bears defensive end Richard Dent, was the 203rd pick in the 1983 draft.

Others succeeded in spite of onerous burdens they lugged into the Big Game. We refer, of course, to Kansas City quarterback Len Dawson's legal problems (Supe IV), Steelers quarterback Terry Bradshaw's insomnia (XIV) and 49ers wide receiver Jerry Rice's bum ankle (XXIII). The more you learn about Super Bowl heroes, the more you realize that with the possi-

Even the supremely talented Troy Aikman (right) had obstacles to overcome on the path to Super Bowl greatness.

Perhaps more than any other player, Montana—Joe Cool indeed—made Super Bowl success appear effortless.

While McGee (above left) weathered a major-league hangover en route to his heroics in Super Bowl I, Plunkett (above right) had to endure a trip to the waiver wire before emerging as the Raiders' Super Bowl savior.

ble exception of Montana, nothing came easily to any of them. Even Dallas quarterback Troy Aikman, with his supernatural arm and matinee-idol's name, was pigeon-toed as a toddler and had to wear orthopedic shoes. "Nothing is given to anyone in life," Aikman has said, although twice drawing the snakebitten Buffalo Bills as a Super Bowl opponent is, he might admit, something of a gift.

But the point is that great ones make their own breaks. Late in the 1982 season Washington running back John Riggins set the stage for his own postseason eruption, essentially commanding Redskins coach Joe Gibbs to give him the ball more often. When

Raiders halfback Marcus Allen took a Plunkett handoff in Supe XVII and saw too many Redskins, he scrapped the play, reversed his field and sprinted into the history books with a 74-yard touchdown dash.

Allen played for 14 more years and never reached the Super Bowl again. That one broken-field run is the play for which he will be best remembered, the play strangers are forever asking him to recount; forever telling him where they were watching from when he crossed the goal line. The power of the game is such that those who excel in the Super Bowl become household words, their feats a kind of national currency. This is their reward, and their punishment.

Joe **Montana**

The Genius was expounding on his most brilliant pupil. "Leadership comes from competence," San Francisco 49ers coach Bill Walsh told a banquet hall full of Rotarians in 1982. "Joe Montana became a leader, at first, because of his feet and his arm. Leadership is by example, not talk."

Without further talk, then, let us relive a few examples of Niners quarterback Montana's peerless leadership:

• Dec. 7, 1980: A day that will live in infamy … for certain New Orleans Saints and their fans. In his second NFL start, Montana rallied the San Francisco 49ers from a 35–7 halftime deficit to a 38–35 win. He still had plenty of outrageously implausible comebacks left in him.

• Jan. 10, 1982: The Catch! Dwight Clark levitated, it seemed, forever, before coming down with Montana's desperation pass to beat the Cowboys in the NFC title game. "The difference," declared Dallas coach Tom Landry, whose Cowboys had grown accustomed to knocking the Niners around, "is Montana."

Two weeks later Montana was voted the MVP of his team's 26–21 win over the Cincinnati Bengals in Super Bowl XVI. Late in that game, with the 49ers clinging to a six-point lead and needing a first down, Montana sprinted to his right and hit receiver Mike Wilson for a 22-yard gain. "Joe is one of the greatest who ever played at doing that," said Walsh of Montana's ability to hurry out of the pocket and throw on a dead run with pinpoint accuracy. Receivers marveled at and became spoiled by Montana's ability to hit them in stride, to put the ball where it would be most catchable for them and least so for defenders.

• Jan. 20, 1985: Montana won his second Super Bowl MVP award, completing 24 of 35 passes for 331 yards and three touchdowns against the Miami Dolphins in Supe XIX.

• Nov. 9, 1986: Less than two months after surgery to widen his spinal canal and remove a ruptured disk, he was named NFC offensive player of the week for completing 13 of 19 passes for 270 yards and three touchdowns in the Niners' 43–17 victory over St. Louis. He was built like the paperboy, but tough as a steel-toed boot.

• Sept. 20, 1987: Cincinnati couldn't quite run all the time off the clock. Montana hit Jerry Rice with the game-winning touchdown pass with no time left. San Francisco won the regular-season game, 27–26. Montana tormented the Bengals like no other team. We are thinking of Supe XVI, and, of course, of …

• Jan. 22, 1989: Joe Cool at his coolest, leading an 11-play, 92-yard, Super Bowl XXIII-winning drive against the Bengals. He fired a 10-yard touchdown pass to receiver John Taylor with 34 seconds left on the clock to put the Niners ahead 20–16. "There have been, and will be, much better arms and legs, and much better bodies on quarterbacks in the NFL," San Francisco lineman Randy Cross once said. "But if you have to win a game or score a touchdown or win a championship, the only guy to get is Joe Montana."

• Jan. 28, 1990: Sheer dominance and little drama as the Niners beat the Broncos 55–10 in Supe XXIV. Montana threw five TD passes and won his third Super Bowl–MVP award.

• April '93: The Kansas City Chiefs traded for the 36-year-old Montana, who led them to within a game of the Super Bowl the following season.

Joe Cool retired after the '94 season and was accorded a bash in San Francisco that would have embarrassed a head of state. The essence of the occasionally tiresome testimonials that poured forth that day was that Montana's career had transcended athletics, had been something historic. We'll give him that. To see this guy play was to know in one's bones that he was a once-in-a-lifetime talent.

Bart **Starr**

How much did the Green Bay Packers think of their rookie quarterback, Bart Starr, the kid out of Alabama with the apocryphal sounding name and the truly bad back? They thought so much of him that they snapped him up in the 17th round of the 1956 draft. They thought so much of him that they assigned him jersey No. 42 during training camp. They weren't trying to convert him to defensive back, either.

"It was obvious," said Starr, "they thought I was not going to stay."

Starr had injured his back punting, of all things, at Alabama, and was used sparingly his last two years in college. In the Packers' camp, though, the southerner was a surprise. Never strong of arm, Starr nonetheless impressed the Green Bay coaching staff with his accuracy and acumen. He made the team as a rookie, and was still around in '59 when Vince Lombardi arrived. After studying lots of film, the new coach decided that he liked Starr's mechanics and would build his team around him.

It mattered little to Lombardi that Starr's arm was not a cannon. The bespectacled future legend eschewed blitzes and bombs alike. Blitzes were for "weaklings" and the long pass was a risky, get-rich-quick scheme, a tacit admission of some lack of fundamental soundness. Starr's smarts and pinpoint accuracy made him an ideal quarterback for his coach's ball-control offense.

In 1960, Starr led the Packers to the first of six division titles they would win in the '60s. He was named the NFL's MVP in 1966 and was also the MVP of the first two Super Bowls, but never earned (or sought) the renown achieved by many of his teammates. While wide receiver Max McGee was breaking curfew and running back Paul Hornung was sowing his wild oats, Starr was an insurance salesman and a Boy Scout leader. His lack of ego and his smooth efficiency on the field left the impression that he wasn't doing anything difficult. This was an illusion.

"Not much imagination," a rival coach once said of the Packers' attack. "Simple meat-and-potato plays. But it's hard to read Starr. He takes those simple tools and uses them to the hilt."

Certainly there was nothing complicated about the most famous play of Starr's career. Green Bay trailed the Dallas Cowboys 17–14 in the NFL title game in 1967, with 13 seconds to play and the temperature –13° and the ball on the Dallas one. Starr entered the huddle and ... asked for suggestions. "Anybody got anything?"

Silence. Finally, lineman Gale Gillingham volunteered, "Run it between Jerry and Forrest. They'll get it for us." So Starr ran a keeper between right guard Jerry Kramer and right tackle Forrest Gregg to win the game known as the Ice Bowl.

In the inaugural Super Bowl the previous January, the Kansas City Chiefs defended the Pack with a newfangled "stacked" defense designed to take away the run, Chiefs coach Hank Stram having concluded that his best chance of winning would be to make Starr beat them with the pass. Starr obliged, completing 16 of 23 passes for 250 yards and two touchdowns, both to a hungover McGee. The biggest reason for Green Bay's 35–10 win was Starr's ability to convert 10 of 12 third downs into firsts. "We kept trying to change our defensive picture on third down, but he still pierced our areas," said Stram.

The following year, at the age of 33, Starr pierced the areas of the Oakland Raiders as Green Bay coasted to a 33–14 victory in the second Super Bowl. He would play another four seasons for the Pack, who retired his number—15, not 42—in 1973. He was inducted into the Hall of Fame in 1977. Not bad for a 17th-rounder with limited tools.

Terry **Bradshaw**

Has an athlete ever been so successful and still caught so much grief? Pittsburgh Steelers quarterback Terry Bradshaw won four Super Bowls in a six-year span, was twice named MVP of the Big Game, and called his own plays throughout, often brilliantly. Yet he was widely and unfairly judged to have had more natural ability than brain power.

"I guess every quarterback has an image," Bradshaw said in 1978, a few weeks before winning his third Super Bowl. "Pat Haden is too short, Roger Staubach is too clean, and I'm too dumb. I could get a doctorate in chemical engineering and they'd call me dumb. I just can't fight it any longer."

He would win the important battles, though there were times during his rookie season when one wondered if he would win anything at all. On Jan. 9, 1970, the wretched Steelers and the suck-out-loud Chicago Bears flipped a coin for the right to select Bradshaw, an effervescent quarterback out of Louisiana Tech, with the first pick of the draft. The Steelers won the coin toss and, with the Shreveport native at the helm, took only five games the following season. His numbers—six touchdown passes against 24 interceptions; a 38.1 completion percentage—were as brutal as his social life.

"I lived in a little apartment out near the airport that first year," Bradshaw said. "God, it was horrible. I'd go home every night and it was me and Johnny Carson. Pathetic. I'd think so much I'd start to cry. My confidence got so bad, I called my college coach and asked him to send me up some reels from my senior year, so I could try to get it back."

Despite marked improvement his next two seasons, in '74 he was beaten out for the starting job during training camp by Joe Gilliam. He won the job back midway through the season, which ended with Pittsburgh's 16–6 win over the Minnesota Vikings in Super Bowl IX. Although Bradshaw threw the winning touchdown pass, it was a game dominated by game-MVP running back Franco Harris and Pittsburgh's Steel Curtain defense.

In the fourth quarter of the following Super Bowl, against the Dallas Cowboys, Bradshaw dealt a blow to the national image of him as a slow-witted man, or, in his words, "a Bible-totin' Li'l Abner." Detecting a safety blitz, he changed the play at the line of scrimmage, then hit Lynn Swann in stride with a touchdown pass that traveled at least 70 yards in the air. It was Bradshaw's final play of the game, which the Steelers won 21–17. He was knocked cold by the Dallas blitz as he released the pass.

The Steelers returned to the Super Bowl after the '78 season, to that point the finest of Bradshaw's career. New rules designed to open up the passing game had been instituted during the off-season, and Steelers head coach Chuck Noll unhesitatingly put his team's fate in the hands of the maturing Bradshaw.

The increased responsibility suited the increasingly bald quarterback fine: "I was chomping at the bit," he said. "I wanted to open it up." Though he was hardly a spectator in the Steelers' first two Super Bowl seasons, Bradshaw's importance nonetheless increased dramatically in the latter half of the Steeler dynasty. In Super Bowls XIII and XIV he threw for a combined 627 yards and six touchdowns. He also won the MVP awards in those victories over the Cowboys and Rams, respectively.

Eight division titles, four NFL championships. All because Ed McCaskey, son-in-law of Chicago Bears founder George Halas, had stood in a ballroom in New Orleans's Fairmont Hotel on Jan. 9, 1970, and said, "Heads," as the 1921 silver dollar tossed by NFL Commissioner Pete Rozelle reached its apex.

Rozelle's call came a moment later: "Tails it is."

Jerry **Rice**

It was three in the morning and someone—a prowler?—was in the garage. Turns out it was the owner of the home, San Francisco 49ers wide receiver Jerry Rice. Having decided the plaster cast on his left leg had served its purpose, Rice was now cutting it off with a hacksaw. Ex-49ers linebacker Jack (Hacksaw) Reynolds had earned his nickname by sawing a car in half; what Rice was doing seemed about as sensible.

Three weeks earlier, the best wide receiver—arguably the best offensive player—in football history, had undergone reconstructive surgery to repair a torn posterior medial capsule and strained medial collateral ligaments in his left knee. Possibly career-ending, definitely season-ending: That was the word on Rice's injury. And for an ordinary player, it might have been.

But on Dec. 15, 1997, just 15 weeks after Rice went down, he took the field against the Denver Broncos. His second-quarter touchdown catch in that game, however, turned out to be his final play of the season: Rice fractured his left kneecap upon impact with the end zone turf in 3Com Park.

No one doubted that he would be back. Rice applies the same extraordinary effort to his rehabilitation that he does to his off-season conditioning. No one in the NFL, possibly no one in sports, works harder at his job than Rice. Which is half the reason no one is likely to match his career numbers. Before the '97 season he'd had 11 1,000-yard receiving seasons; he has 166 (and counting) career touchdowns, the most in NFL history.

But early in his career there was a discordant note in the symphony of superlatives. Rice had not scored a touchdown in the first three playoff games of his career, and when San Francisco qualified for the playoffs after the '88 season, Rice's fourth NFL season, the whispers began—*think Rice'll show up this time?* Rest

assured that this extremely proud man heard the whispers.

He also silenced them. In the two playoff games before Supe XXIII against the Cincinnati Bengals, Rice caught nine passes for 159 yards and five touchdowns. When Rice turned his right ankle in a workout before the big game, it was huge news, until the word got out that Rice went out dancing three nights after the injury. Still, Niners coach Bill Walsh insisted the injury worried him; Walsh was trying to take pressure off Rice, who was playing in his first Super Bowl.

Walsh needn't have worried. Rice pulled down 11 passes for a Super Bowl-record 215 yards. He caught a 14-yard pass for a touchdown in the fourth quarter, but none of his catches was more clutch than one he produced on second-and-20 from the Cincinnati 45-yard-line later in the game. Niners quarterback Joe Montana called a square-in to Rice, who was triple-teamed. "It had to be a perfect throw and catch," recalled Bengals free safety Ray Horton.

It was both, and it resulted in a 27-yard gain that set up the game-winning touchdown. The Bengals were so concerned about Rice that several plays later Montana was able to hit Rice's receiving partner John Taylor in the end zone. The 49ers won the game, 20–16; Rice was the MVP. Although he would star in two subsequent Super Bowl wins—with a total of 28 catches for 512 yards, this product of tiny Mississippi Valley State is the leading receiver in the history of the Big Game—Super Bowl XXIII remains his most memorable performance.

"We didn't do a bad job on him," said Cincinnati strong safety David Fulcher of Rice. "He only got one touchdown." The Bengals had allowed Rice 11 catches for 215 yards and a touchdown, and now they were saying, *Hey, against Rice, we'll take that*. It was not so much a surrender as a measure of the excellence of the best receiver in Super Bowl history.

Joe **Namath**

The trappings and symbols were piled on so thick and heavy that they tended to hide the real guy. Read enough about the llama-skin rug and marble bar and oval bed in New York Jets quarterback Joe Namath's apartment, hear enough about his Fu Manchu mustache and $427,000 contract and pantyhose commercial, and it is possible to forget that Namath was just a tough, fun-loving kid from western Pennsylvania playing on bad knees and speaking his mind.

Entertainment mogul and Jets owner Sonny Werblin had thrown all that jack at him because the kid had star power, and Namath understood that. In the days before Super Bowl III, when Namath was told over and over that the Baltimore Colts were prohibitive favorites to beat the Jets, what was he supposed to say? *They're a great team. It will be an honor just to be on the field with them.*

To hell with that. Three days before the game, Namath guaranteed a victory for his team and his league, the maligned, upstart AFL. While his fellow Jets fed off Namath's confidence, the rest of the world wasn't so sure. As the day of the game drew nigh, Vegas fattened the spread, moving the Colts from 17 to 19½ point favorites. As one NFL coach said before the kickoff, "Namath plays in his first pro game today."

The smug, older league, lopsided winner of the first two Super Bowls, was due a comeuppance. After reviewing film of Baltimore's secondary, Jets coach Weeb Ewbank had come to a conclusion: "They're slow. If we can't pass on these guys we ought to get out of the business." He didn't have to convince Namath, who turned to a teammate after pregame warmups and said, "My arm is so loose it feels like it's going to fall off." Kind of how his tongue must have felt all the time.

The longest pass he threw all day was an early, incomplete

bomb to a streaking wide receiver Don Maynard, which "put the fear of God in them for the rest of the game," Namath said. It also opened things up for wide receiver George Sauer, who would catch eight passes for 133 yards.

Decent numbers, as were those amassed by fullback Matt Snell, who rushed for 121 yards on 30 carries. But the MVP Award in the most amazing game in the history of professional football—Jets 16, Colts 7—went to Namath. It had to. He won the award partly because he completed 17 of his 28 passes for 206 yards and partly because he was the guy who'd sat in a chaise longue poolside the day before the game and told reporters that the Jets were about to take pro football's status quo and set it on its ear.

This was the year the Super Bowl doubled as an allegory: the AFL's Jets as Haight-Ashbury, the NFL's Colts as U.S. Steel. Namath's personality was big enough to accommodate everything that accompanied such an historic win. Here was a guy who socialized with Dean Martin, Frank Sinatra and Toots Shor. When his chum Howard Cosell dropped by for a visit, Namath's roommate, Jets safety Ray Abruzzese, groggily emerged from a bedroom. "I thought you were the TV," he said to Cosell. "I was coming out to turn you off."

In 1973, Namath was told by reporters that he had made Richard Nixon's enemies list. A lot of people who witnessed Namath's brash playboy act agreed with Nixon. By calling his shot before Super Bowl III, Namath contributed incalculable credibility to the AFL, which merged with the NFL in 1970. It turned out to be a pretty good move for both, wouldn't you say? Regardless of how the establishment felt about him, in the end, Namath was the NFL's friend.

Lynn **Swann**

The defining game of Lynn Swann's career was a testament both to his courage and to the restorative powers of a nap.

Swann showed up at Miami's Orange Bowl for Super Bowl X against the Dallas Cowboys two hours before the rest of the Steelers. Using his gym bag as a pillow, he stretched out on the floor of the dressing room and caught some z's. He arose, he later recalled, refreshed and "ready to play, ready to show the Dallas Cowboys and everyone else that Lynn Swann can't be intimidated."

In just his second season, the wide receiver out of Southern Cal was on the verge of superstardom. Unable to cover Swann, a 25-foot long-jumper in high school, NFL defensive backs had entered into an unofficial contest to see which of them could be the first to knock his head off. In the fourth game of that 1975 season, against the Denver Broncos, a former Steelers cornerback named John Rowser, a.k.a. Dirty John, had repeatedly mugged Swann. For the rest of the season, defensive backs around the league followed suit. The thuggery sunk to new depths in the AFC title game, in which Oakland Raiders safety Jack Tatum left his feet, far from the play, to club Swann in the back of the head. That dazed Swann, but Tatum had just been softening him up for fellow defensive back George Atkinson, whose headhunting tackle after a Swann reception put the receiver in the hospital with a severe concussion.

No one knew if he would play in the Super Bowl. Swann practiced once, the day before the game, and dropped everything thrown to him. His gait was stiff, his timing off. "When Cliff Harris started talking so much," Swann said later, "that's when I knew I was going to play."

Harris, a Cowboys safety, had spent the week telling Swann, through the media, that if he cared about his health, he should probably take Sunday off. Had Swann not played, the Steelers would have one Vince Lombardi Trophy fewer in their lobby.

Coming out of his catnap, though, Swann felt like a million bucks. He caught just four passes in the game, but three of those catches belonged in the Louvre.

Catch 1: Has been called the most amazing in Super Bowl history, and is mentioned elsewhere in this book, but bears repeating. With his momentum carrying him out of bounds, Swann contorted his body and reached inside the arms of Dallas cornerback Mark Washington, made the grab and somehow defied physics to get his feet in bounds. The play went 32 yards and set up Pittsburgh's first touchdown.

Catch 2: The one everyone remembers. Wearing Washington like a cape, Swann juggled Terry Bradshaw's 53-yard rainbow before gathering it, at last, while lying on the ground. Didn't lead to any points but was well worth the price of admission to Super Bowl X.

Catch 4: Game-winning 64-yard bomb came after Swann abandoned his pattern and outran his coverage. "No moves, no fakes, just straight-ahead juice," he said.

Swann was named the game's MVP and, having already incurred two serious concussions, came very close to retiring in the off-season, at the age of 25. He decided that to do so would be to concede victory to the men who sought to intimidate him. So he stuck around for another seven years, torturing defensive backs and winning two more Super Bowls. He hauled in 12 passes and scored two touchdowns in those last two championship games, playing brilliantly but never so memorably as the day he awakened from his nap and put the Cowboys to sleep.

Jim **Plunkett**

If your memories of Jim Plunkett's heroics are hazy, that could be because he was a certified public accountant among Hell's Angels, a reserved, softspoken player amid the wing nuts and wackos who comprised the Raiders. In another sense he was a typical member of the Silver and Black: Before reaching the peak of his profession, earning the MVP award for his performance in the Raiders 27–10 win over the Philadelphia Eagles in Super Bowl XV, Plunkett had been at the bottom. Unloaded by the Patriots and the 49ers before Raiders owner Al Davis claimed him off the waiver wire, Plunkett was the quintessential Raider reclamation project.

It was not until his second NFL season that things went bad for this son of a blind news vendor. That's when New England Patriots head coach Chuck Fairbanks came up with a brilliant idea and summoned Plunkett to his office. *Guess what,* Fairbanks told his quarterback, *You're going to run the option!*

Fairbanks had apparently forgotten that he was no longer coaching in the Big Eight. The 1970 Heisman winner as a drop-back passer at Stanford, Plunkett could scramble some, but, at 6' 2", 215 pounds, he was not your prototypical wishbone wizard. Not surprisingly, Plunkett took a pounding in that second season, suffering a series of back and shoulder injuries that would plague him throughout his career.

Subsequent seasons brought more injuries and, Plunkett admitted, less confidence. In '76 the Patriots traded him to the 49ers, who gave up on him two seasons later. He was contemplating retirement, another washed up ex-Heisman winner, when Davis forked over the $100 waiver fee for his rights.

A backup in his first two seasons with Oakland, Plunkett got the call five games into the '80 season. The Raiders had started out a disappointing 2–3, and starting quarterback Dan Pastorini broke his leg in a Game 5 loss to the Kansas City Chiefs. With Plunkett calling the signals, the Raiders won their next six games and 13 of their next 15 including playoffs.

Plunkett was something of a wallflower, but then, with defensive back Lester Hayes (he of the "stickum"-lathered forearms), defensive end John (Tooz) Matuszak and linebacker Ted (the Mad Stork) Hendricks, the last thing the 1980 Raiders needed was another "character". Someone needed to stay cool, defensive end Howie Long said, and Plunkett "set that tone for the whole team."

He engineered his first touchdown pass against the Eagles in Super Bowl XV by coolly stepping up in the pocket to freeze Philly corner Herman Edwards and linebacker John Bunting, then hitting receiver Cliff Branch for a two-yard touchdown pass. Plunkett would hit Branch again for 29 yards and a touchdown, but this game's offensive highlight was Plunkett's second scoring pass of the day, an 80-yarder to running back Kenny King. The trophies Plunkett won that season told the story of his career's peaks and valleys: they were for the Super Bowl MVP and the NFL's comeback player of the year.

Three years later he played a less spectacular but still integral role in the Raiders' rout of the Washington Redskins in Super Bowl XVIII. His teammates valued his steadying presence. Long once told a reporter that Plunkett gave his team the "El Cid factor—in the final scene, they're outnumbered 20–1, the castle is surrounded. Then they prop up Charlton Heston's beat-up body on a horse, and the opposing army retreats at the sight of him."

The difference was that in the movie El Cid had expired before being propped up on that horse; Plunkett, before joining the Raiders, had merely been given up for dead.

Larry **Csonka**

By the end of his career it was spread out over an unnaturally wide area on his face and resembled not so much a nose as the side of an alp. In addition to breaking his schnoz a dozen times in the line of duty, Miami Dolphins fullback Larry Csonka incurred numerous concussions, a cracked eardrum, plus knee and elbow injuries that frequently required surgery. Making it easier for Csonka to endure the pain was the knowledge that he gave as good as he got.

If such a place could be said to exist, Csonka occupied a soft spot in the heart of Miami Dolphins coach Don Shula, and not just because of their shared Hungarian heritage, or the fact that Csonka fumbled only 21 times in 1,997 carries during his 11-year NFL career. For the two seasons in the early 1970s that the Dolphins kicked sand in the face of the entire league, winning 32 of 34 games and a pair of Super Bowls, they relied on a ball-control attack that called for a running play on two of every three snaps. The centerpiece to that assault was the man they called Zonk, a 6' 3", 235-pound blunt instrument of a fullback behind whom the Dolphins bludgeoned their way to greatness.

But at the beginning of his career, Zonk had a slight problem, namely that he led with his head. He suffered a series of concussions which sidelined him for six games in his first two seasons, in '68 and '69. To conserve grey matter, Csonka took to wearing a special, water-filled helmet, and to leading with his forearm.

He eventually ditched the special helmet, and started wearing his old one with the suspension shifted forward so that that the headgear sat menacingly low on his brow. "All I can see is your mustache," Chiefs linebacker Willie Lanier once said. "Good," replied Csonka. "I'd just as soon you didn't know which hole I'm looking at."

Not that Csonka needed one. Said Dolphins halfback Jim Kiick, "I like to run where there's holes, Larry likes to run where there's people."

He especially liked to run when the games meant something. In Super Bowl VII, Zonk overpowered the Washington Redskins with 112 yards on only 15 carries, helping the Dolphins complete the only perfect season in NFL history. Against the Raiders in the following season's AFC title game, he piled up 117 yards and three touchdowns, causing Oakland head coach John Madden to despair, "What do you do against Csonka? The longer the day gets, the better he is, the more he hurts you."

Zonk turned in the finest game of his Hall of Fame career a fortnight later, bulling for 145 yards and two touchdowns in Miami's easy win over Minnesota in Supe VIII. So dominant was the Dolphins' ground game in that contest that quarterback Bob Griese needed to throw only seven passes.

After a brief hiatus in the short-lived World Football League, Csonka played three years with the New York Giants before returning to Miami for a farewell season in '79. "He hasn't lost a damn thing!" proclaimed center Jim Langer after an early season game.

If that was the case, Csonka got out before he had to, after the '79 season. Years later, he talked about the wages of his brutal style of play. "The first thing I do when I get out of bed and feel the jolt in my knees is think of Roy Winston. On the second step, my calcified Adam's apple starts bobbing, and I think of Carl Eller. A few more steps in the dark and it's Willie Lanier. By the time I get to the bathroom I'm flashing back to Dick Butkus and Ray Nitschke. And when the light finally comes on, I just hope that somewhere in the darkness they're thinking of me, too."

Randy White (left) and Harvey Martin

Randy White & Harvey Martin

Humble beginnings? You want humble beginnings? Dallas Cowboys defensive tackle Randy White played on a high school team that won five games in two years, and as a senior, he failed to make first-team all-state. "In Delaware," said White. He arrived at the University of Maryland as a 210-pound fullback and was told to switch positions and put on weight.

Dallas defensive end Harvey Martin was so scared and bashful a youth that he once stood idly by while his sister thrashed a high school bully who'd been picking on him. "Good job," he said when she finished. So tentative and frightened was Martin during his first season of football, as a junior, that his coach told the team he looked like "a dying calf in a hailstorm."

Although Martin improved quickly, only a heroic selling job—by that same coach—got him a scholarship at East Texas State, where one of his teammates was the future Pittsburgh Steeler Dwight White. "He was a big Baby Huey," White recalled. "He was so gentle, small guys used him as an ego-builder. Everybody borrowed money off him. He was more or less a chump."

On Jan. 15, 1978, the former shrimp and the ex-chump arrived simultaneously at the pinnacle of their shared profession. Spearheading a defense that forced eight turnovers in the Dallas Cowboys 27–10 win over the Denver Broncos in Super Bowl XII, Martin and White were named co-MVPs, the first—and as of 1998 the only—players to share the award. Beautiful Harvey and the Manster, as they were known, sacked Broncos quarterback Craig Morton once apiece and pressured him into throwing four interceptions, which equaled, incidentally, the number of passes the overwhelmed Morton completed in 15 attempts.

White was then finishing up his first full season as a defensive tackle; it took the Dallas braintrust two years to abandon their fantasies of making him a middle linebacker (which explained White's anomalous number, 54). He would go on to make All-Pro nine straight times and earn the distinctive nickname coined by teammates who described him as half-man, half-monster.

The trajectory of the Manster's career was still on the ascent at Supe XII, while Martin's was at its apex. The radio show he hosted was called The Beautiful Harvey Martin Show. And why not? His life *was* beautiful. In his fifth NFL season he had 85 tackles and 23 sacks—a year that, because of the league's subsequent redefinition of what constitutes holding, is unlikely to ever be reproduced. He was an All-Pro, the defensive player of the year, owner of a Super Bowl ring and a Super Bowl MVP trophy. It doesn't get much better than that.

And for Martin, it didn't. He played another six seasons, with distinction. But while his sack totals remained in double digits—he had 16, 10, 12 and 10 over the next four years—he never again approached the level of his Super season. In '81 coach Tom Landry relieved him of his defensive captaincy and gave it to White, for whom Martin held no bitterness afterward. In August '82, Martin's name arose in connection with a drug investigation by the Dallas police department. Martin was never arrested and he recalled that White was the only teammate who stood by him.

They had stood side by side before. Beautiful Harvey and the Manster were linked by friendship and also by the events of Jan. 15, 1978, when they stood together in the Superdome, at the peak of their profession.

John **Stallworth**

A few days before the Steelers won their fourth Super Bowl, Pittsburgh receiver John Stallworth was zigzagging through a press conference, muttering apologies and excuse-me's, when he stumbled over a tripod that held a spotlight that was focused on Lynn Swann, his teammate and fellow wide receiver. How appropriate. During their nine seasons together, the spotlight was almost always trained on Swann while Stallworth, despite lighting up Super Bowls XIII and XIV, toiled in relative darkness. In the public mind they seemed to be the Swann and the ugly duckling. Swann was drafted in the first round out of high-gloss Southern Cal. Stallworth was plucked out of Division II Alabama A&M in the fourth round. Swann blossomed early, while Stallworth was not considered his equal as a receiver until the late 1970s.

"Even now, when I think of the two of them, I think of Swann," says ex-Washington Redskins wide receiver Bobby Mitchell. "But when it was over, Stallworth was the guy who killed you."

Make no mistake, Swann deserved the spotlight, but he could have shared it with Stallworth. When Stallworth's career was over he owned every significant Steelers career receiving record. He retired after the '87 season, having played five more years than Swann. He is the leading play-off receiver in NFL history with 12 touchdown catches, three in Super Bowls. His career was characterized by sustained excellence and, when it mattered most, bursts of brilliance. His yards-per-catch average in four Super Bowls was 24.4; his yards-per-touchdown-catch average in those Super Bowls was a whopping 58.7 yards. Take away Stallworth's explosions in Supes XIII and XIV and the Steelers are hard-pressed to win. Without Stallworth, perhaps their dynasty is downgraded to a nice short run.

Raised in Tuscaloosa but spurned by the University of Alabama, Stallworth was accustomed to disappointment. As a high school running back, Stallworth was skinny and, in Bear Bryant's opinion, ran too upright. After being a

non-factor in Pittsburgh's first two Super victories, however, he diplomatically voiced his wish that quarterback Terry Bradshaw would look his way more often. When the NFL stacked the deck against defenses in '78 and the Steelers began airing it out, Bradshaw looked his way plenty.

Against the Cowboys in the first quarter of the '79 Super Bowl, Stallworth threw a head fake that spun Dallas cornerback Aaron Kyle around like a figure skater, then caught Bradshaw's 28-yard touchdown lob. After Dallas had scored 14 unanswered points, Stallworth wrested the momentum back from them when he gathered in a 10-yard completion, broke the tackle of Kyle—who had a long first half—and went 75 yards for another touchdown. And then to Kyle's vast relief Stallworth was basically done, sidelined by leg cramps. His day's work: three catches, 115 yards, two TDs.

Against the Los Angeles Rams in Supe XIV it was Swann's turn to exit early, having landed hard on his head after skying to bring down a Bradshaw pass. On third-and-eight on his own 27-yard line, trailing 19–17 with a little more than 12 minutes to play, Bradshaw called 60 Prevent Slot Hook and Go. Stallworth's assignment was to curl back toward the line of scrimmage, get the cornerback to bite on the move, then head for the hills. He sold the fake, split two Rams defensive backs and scored on a 73-yard play. Two series later he caught a 45-yard bomb—this catch was shorter but more acrobatic—only to be tackled at the 22-yard line. A one-yard Franco Harris smash five plays later put the finishing touch on Pittsburgh's 31–19 win.

Afterward, forlorn Rams cornerback Rod Perry, the burn victim on Stallworth's game-winning touchdown, said "I did the best I could. Hey, haven't you ever seen a perfect play?"

Bradshaw was named the MVP and linebacker Jack Lambert, whose interception snuffed L.A.'s final drive, was the late-game hero. But Perry could have told you: Stallworth was the guy who killed them.

Franco **Harris**

He was smart, but not omniscient, and who knows how things would have worked out if Chuck Noll had gotten his way? The 1972 season was looming and the Pittsburgh Steelers needed a feature running back. Noll, the head coach, liked Robert Newhouse, a 5'10" fireplug out of Houston. Noll was in the minority.

Art Rooney Jr., the Steelers' vice president in charge of personnel, and most of the Steelers scouts liked Penn State's Franco Harris, who at 6'2", 225 pounds was nearly as big as many of the Pittsburgh offensive linemen who would be opening holes for him. The choice of Harris wasn't a no-brainer: He'd played in the shadow of running back Lydell Mitchell in college; his 40-yard-dash time of 4.7 seconds was mediocre for a halfback. During his senior year he'd been briefly suspended by Nittany Lions head coach Joe Paterno for being late to practice. It was a hard sell, but Art Jr. finally convinced Noll to take the bigger back, foibles and all.

Harris became an instant favorite among success-starved Steelers fans whose team had gone 6–8 in '71 and had not won a title of any kind in 40 years of existence. Running the weakside sweeps that would become the signature of his Hall-of-Fame career, the long-striding half-back rushed for 1,055 yards in his first season, averaging 5.6 yards per carry. In an ethnically diverse city like Pittsburgh, the half-black, half-Italian Harris was both star and microcosm of his new hometown.

Up sprang Harris's distinctive fan club, Franco's Italian Army, which late in the season added to its ranks a certain well known Italian-American from Hoboken, N.J. In the week before their division-clinching win in San Diego, the Steelers trained in Palm Springs. On the invitation of Steelers radio announcer Myron Cope, who passed him a note on a napkin at a restaurant, Frank Sinatra showed up at a

Steelers practice in midweek and was commissioned as a one-star general in Franco's "Army." Provolone was consumed, red wine sipped. In addition to winning the NFL's rookie-of-the-year award, Cope recalled, "Harris became the first player in the history of the league to drink during practice."

It usually took Harris a series or two to get into the flow of a game. So it was appropriate that the most memorable play of this slow-starter's career came in the final minute of a critical contest. With 22 seconds on the clock and fourth-and-long standing between the Steelers and the off-season, Harris plucked a Terry Bradshaw pass off his shoestrings after the ball had ricocheted off Oakland Raiders safety Jack Tatum. He clutched the wayward ball and rumbled 42 yards for the game-winning touchdown, giving Pittsburgh its first-ever playoff win. Though it did not occur in a Super Bowl, the Immaculate Reception, as the improbable catch became known, is widely regarded as the play that propelled Pittsburgh out of the doldrums.

"Franco was the guy who lifted the Steelers to a new plateau," All-Pro defensive tackle Mean Joe Greene once said. "He made us believe we could win." The first time Pittsburgh won it all, beating the Vikings 16–6 in Super Bowl IX, Harris rushed for 158 yards and a touchdown and was named MVP. Always a money performer, he would go on to score 17 touchdowns and rush for 1,556 yards in 19 career postseason games. In Pittsburgh's four Super Bowl wins, he scored 24 points and rushed for a Super Bowl-record 354 yards.

Harris played 12 seasons in Pittsburgh and—after a contract squabble with the Rooneys—a final one in Seattle. And though Robert Newhouse had a nice career for the Dallas Cowboys, no one could doubt that on that fateful spring day in '72, the Steelers had chosen the right back.

Steve **Young**

San Francicso 49ers quarterback Steve Young makes our list because on Jan. 29, 1995, he threw a record six touchdown passes in Super Bowl XXIX, a game that was over before all the spectators at Joe Robbie Stadium had taken their seats. And he makes it because it gives us pleasure to thumb our noses at all those spoiled San Francisco 49ers fans who refused to accept Young for no other reason than that he wasn't Joe Montana.

No, he wasn't. During their uneasy six-year coexistence in the Bay Area, Young's behavior, unlike Montana's, was consistently classy. While Montana sniped at and disparaged his longtime understudy, at one point referring to Young as "the enemy," and saying, "Steve's on a big push for himself," Young had only good things to say about his rival. His reward? After Young led the 49ers to a 14–2 record in '92—a season Montana missed with elbow trouble—and was voted the MVP of the league, a poll conducted by a Bay Area radio station showed that 75 percent of respondents favored dumping him and retaining Montana.

Listening with both ears, apparently, was 49ers owner Eddie DeBartolo, who in the off-season offered Montana his old job back, meaning that the NFL's reigning MVP would be a backup. Montana rejected the offer, and was traded to the Kansas City Chiefs. Still, the 49ers' ingratitude to Young and lack of confidence in him must have rankled.

Ever the gentleman, Young stuck steadfastly to the high road, saying only positive things about 49ers management and Montana, in whose absence he flourished. In '93 Young led the league in passing for the third straight season, only to see his team lose to the Cowboys in the NFC title game for the second year in a row. His vindication would have to wait another year.

His season of redemption was marked, surprisingly, by a temper tantrum. On Oct. 2, 1994, after being yanked from a game the 49ers were losing badly, Young stood on the sideline and screamed at head coach George Seifert. While it was widely postulated that this uncharacteristic display of emotion earned the respect of his teammates, the fact was, their respect was already his. He'd earned it earlier in the season by repeatedly and uncomplainingly scraping himself off the turf behind a patchwork offensive line.

As his starting linemen trickled back that season, Young began his ascent to The Zone. He finished with 35 touchdowns against ten interceptions. His passer rating of 112.8 surpassed Montana's '89 season as the best ever recorded.

Late in the season, with his second MVP all but wrapped up, Young was asked to take the long view of his career, of the years spent in Montana's shadow and a city's puzzling reluctance to take him in. Said Young, "There was a long time when I'd get up in the morning and say, 'What do I do today? Nothing really easy is happening here, so I'll work through it.' In the end, it didn't kill me. It made me stronger. This year I've enjoyed playing football more than I ever thought I could."

It got better. A month after making that assessment Young threw half a dozen touchdown passes against the overmatched San Diego Chargers, breaking a Super Bowl record held by a certain ex-teammate of his.

The season's de facto Big Game had been two weeks earlier, the Niners' 38–28 win over the Cowboys in the NFC Championship. As Young took a victory lap around Candlestick Park after that breakthrough victory, fans chanted, "Steve! Steve!"

These were the same fans, some of them, who had long refused to embrace Young. They were the same fans, some of them, who did not deserve him.

Emmitt **Smith**

What you had here was a conspicuous lack of awe. Emmitt Smith was impressed, but not wide-eyed. After rushing for 8,800 yards and scoring 106 touchdowns in four years for Escambia High in Pensacola, Fla., Smith won an award from a sports drink company. The prize: an all-expenses-paid trip to Super Bowl XXI in Pasadena. As he stood on the floor of the Rose Bowl and watched Phil Simms shred the Denver Broncos D, Smith turned to John Nichols, his high school coach, whom he had brought as his guest, and declared, "One day, I'm going to play in a game like this."

He was right, of course, and wrong too. As of 1998, Smith had played in—and won—*three* such games. Six years after his first visit he was back in the Rose Bowl, this time rushing for 108 yards in the Dallas Cowboys' 52–17 wipeout of the Buffalo Bills in Super Bowl XXVII. A year after that, Smith carried for 132 yards—91 in the second half—and two touchdowns to win the MVP award in the Cowboys' repeat rout of the Bills.

Which of Dallas's offensive "triplets"—the cloying nickname team owner Jerry Jones coined for Smith, wideout Michael Irvin and quarterback Troy Aikman—is the most indispensible? Jones has gone on record as saying it is Aikman. Others disagree. "If Aikman is out," says New York Giants linebacker Corey Miller, "his replacement can just hand Emmitt the ball and watch his options open up. But if Emmitt is out, defenses can pin their ears back and go after the quarterback. There is no one to replace Emmitt."

Neither a pure power-back nor a breakaway runner, Smith has always defied categorization. When he was coming out of high school, one national recruiting guru wrote, "Emmitt isn't a franchise player. He's a lugger, not a runner. Sportswriters blew him all out of proportion."

Really? In his first start as a freshman at the University of Florida, Smith ran—excuse us, lugged—the ball 39 times for 224 yards, a Gators record. In eight NFL seasons Smith has rushed for 11,234 yards, scored 119 touchdowns and won an NFL MVP award, in addition to his gaudy postseason statistics. He would break the occasional long touchdown run, but Smith in his prime was not so much an open-field back as one of the most reliable movers of the chains in NFL history. His great balance, uncanny vision, and deceptive strength enabled him to break tackles and carry defenders two or three or 10 yards further down the field than seemed possible. "When Emmitt needs to make you miss, he can make anybody miss," said Cowboys guard Nate Newton. "And when he needs to run you over, he can do that too." And he can block like a fullback and catch the ball out of the backfield.

The only question before the 1998–99 season was whether or not he was on the far side of his prime. Smith wasn't much of a factor in the Cowboys' Super Bowl XXX victory, which followed the '95 season. Two weeks after devastating the Packers with 150 rushing yards in the NFC title game, he carried for just 49 yards. In Dallas's three Super seasons in the '90s, Smith averaged 1,657 yards rushing and 4.86 yards-per-carry. In '96 and '97—albeit behind an aging, oft-injured line—that average was down to 3.9.

Clearly, Smith was showing the effects of having had his number called almost 3,000 times in eight years. As the '98 season neared he was unconcerned about his declining numbers. Statistics and records "don't tell you what kind of football player you are," he said. "My talent came from God. What I add is my desire. I have great desire."

Just ask any of the guys who have had to tackle him.

John **Riggins**

He was not always as you remember him in Super Bowl XVII in the Rose Bowl, charging through Hog-vacated holes and scattering Miami Dolphins defenders like ten-pins. When he left the University of Kansas in 1971, John Riggins tipped the scales at well under the 230 pounds he carried in his NFL prime. Sure he ran over people, but that wasn't the extent of his repertoire. He could catch a pass, he could make you miss. "A white Jimmy Brown," is how one scout described him.

A white Dennis Rodman seems more accurate now. Long before the Worm embarked on his postmodern sartorial explorations, Riggins, a New York Jet from 1971–75, was parading around Gotham in leather pants, suspenders, a derby and combat boots. While Rodman was barely in his teens, Riggins blazed a path of tonsorial self-mutilation, alternating between a Mohawk and shaving his head altogether. Raised in Centralia, Kans. (pop. 500), Riggins once explained that his penchant for flakiness derived from a deep-seated need to keep himself amused. Asked by a reporter late in his career whether he was "doing it any better now," he replied, "You'll have to ask my wife."

Riggins could be a world-class wiseass. *Why the Mohawk?* he was asked in '73. "In the off-season I got to observe quite a number of freaks, firsthand," he replied. "I always wondered what it would be like to be treated like one of them."

Displeased with the money the Jets were paying him, he signed as a free agent with the Redskins in '76. He sat out the '80 season in a contract dispute but returned the following season to announce, "I'm bored, I'm broke, and I'm back." Redskins fans did not fully forgive their wayward power back until 1982, when he went into the office of coach Joe Gibbs on the eve of the playoffs and forcefully suggested that the team ride him through the postseason. To his credit, Gibbs obliged. In Washington's three playoff games going into Super Bowl XVII, Riggo had rushed 98 times for 444 yards. And his busiest day lay ahead.

It was off to Pasadena for Super Bowl XVII, but what to wear? As Rodman would have, Riggins packed a number of ensembles. For Wednesday's press conference he opted for guerrilla chic: camouflage pants, army boots and an elephant-gun belt buckle. On Friday he woke up feeling rather more formal, and donned white tie, top hat and tails for Redskins owner Jack Kent Cooke's party. On Sunday he returned to his customary disguise as a truck, running over and around the Miami Dolphins "Killer Bees" defense for 166 yards and a touchdown on 38 carries.

Riggo's 30th carry of the day was the one that broke Miami's spirit. Trailing 17–13 with 11:43 to play, the Redskins faced a fourth-and-one on Miami's 43-yard line. After a timeout, quarterback Joe Theismann returned to the huddle and called 70-Chip—which meant that Riggins would run left behind blocking back Otis Wonsley and Clint Didier, an extra tight end. The play unfolded exactly the way it was drawn up on the chalkboard. The only Dolphin who had a shot at Riggins, cornerback Don McNeal, was repelled as a careless bovine is cast aside by the cowcatcher of a train. Toward the end of his run, Riggins pulled away from Dolphins safety Glenn Blackwood. It was, as one scribe noted, "an astounding show of speed by a 230-pounder on his 30th carry of the day." On Washington's next possession, Riggins carried the ball on eight of 12 snaps to ice the game and lock up the MVP award.

Wit, strength, speed, stamina—Riggins had it all working on this night. The man was a freak.

Phil **Simms**

He was runner-up for NFC rookie of the year in 1979. He threw for 4,044 yards in 1984 and was MVP of the Pro Bowl in '86. But he was not Y.A. Tittle, and for this, Giants fans booed him whenever they could.

It was both a measure of their unrealistic standards and their crankiness at having to navigate the disorienting welter of freeways around Giants Stadium that Giants fans took so long to warm to quarterback Phil Simms.

This continued, incredibly, throughout the '86 season, as Simms led New York to its first division championship in 23 years. On the home stretch of that landmark season, Simms treated the Giants to three come-from-behind wins over playoff-caliber teams—but was still catching heat from the odd moron at the Meadowlands.

"The way to get cheered in New York," Simms concluded, "is to be a backup quarterback. They love backups."

But no Giants fan—no matter how cranky—could have found fault with the clinic Simms conducted in front of the 101,063 people at the Rose Bowl for Super Bowl XXI between the Giants and the Denver Broncos. In the most awesome display of precision passing ever seen in an NFL playoff game, let alone *the* NFL playoff game, Simms completed 22 of 25 passes for 268 yards and three touchdowns. By completing 88 percent of his throws, Simms set a record for passing efficiency in a playoff game that was positively DiMaggioesque. Surely New Yorkers could appreciate that? After dueling with Broncos quarterback John Elway on nearly even terms for a half—after which Denver led, 10–9—Simms pulled away, completing a Super Bowl–record 10 straight passes to start the second half. Elway could not keep pace, and the Giants romped 39–20.

The Giants had an inkling that Simms might make some noise. The eight-year veteran out of Morehead State was so sharp in a practice nine days before the Super Bowl that head coach Bill Parcells said to him, "Hey—save something for the game."

The warm weather at the Rose Bowl was a welcome change for Simms. "I was used to throwing in the cold," he recalled, "but now I could grip the ball [better]. I could make it do anything I wanted."

Parcells wanted Simms to get the Broncos off balance by throwing on first down. No problem, coach. The Giants had 12 first-half first downs, and threw on nine of them. Simms completed all nine. Then, in the second half, he got hot. This was the least suspenseful MVP vote in the award's history.

"He quarterbacked as good a game as has ever been played," assessed Parcells, who is not exactly generous in dispensing superlatives. "He was absolutely magnificent."

Simms was still playing terrific ball four years later—he'd led the club to a 12–2 record, and his 108 quarterback rating after Game 10 led the NFL by a dozen points—when he suffered a sprained ligament in his right arch in a game against the Buffalo Bills. Backup Jeff Hostetler quarterbacked the Giants to victory in Supe XXV over the same Bills.

In one of the decisions that would characterize his brief, troubled tenure as successor to the retired Parcells, new Giants coach Ray Handley dubbed Hoss his starter at the beginning of the '90 season. The year after turning in his best statistical season ever, Simms lost his job.

The Giants haven't been close to a Super Bowl since. The day after Handley's bombshell, at the Giants annual preseason luncheon, a crowd of 1,400 stood and cheered Simms for 45 seconds, the longest ovation he ever got in New York.

Simms was right. They love a backup.

Roger **Staubach**

He played in four and won two, and, truth be told, Dallas Cowboys quarterback Roger Staubach was more entertaining in the Super Bowls he lost than in those he won. With the possible exception of John Elway, no quarterback has ever been more dangerous taking the field late in the game with his team in a hole. Staubach could have taught Alan Greenspan a thing or two about erasing a deficit.

Staubach was tenacious and patient because he had to be. Following his graduation from the Naval Academy—where he won the Heisman Trophy as a junior in 1963—Staubach spent four years on active duty, including a year in Vietnam as a supply officer, before joining the Cowboys, who had drafted him in the 10th round in '64.

So he reported to the Cowboys in '69—your basic 27-year-old rookie. Didn't bother Staubach. Throughout his football hiatus he stayed in shape, playing "a lot of basketball and a little tennis and football." Midway through the '71 season, Staubach replaced Craig Morton against Chicago. He lost that game but won the next seven, eventually leading the Cowboys to a suspense-free, 24–3 victory over the Miami Dolphins in Super Bowl V. Staubach's surgical passing in that game—12 for 19, 119 yards and two touchdowns—earned him the game's MVP.

It was the belated beginning of a remarkable run by a first-ballot Hall of Famer. When he retired after the '79 season while still at the top of his game, Staubach had guided his team to four NFC titles and two Super Bowl wins. He had passed for 22,700 yards and 153 touchdowns, and scrambled for another 20 scores—all numbers that might have been greater had Staubach not sacrificed four years in the service of his country.

Six years after his first Super Bowl victory, the 35-year-old Staubach led the Cowboys to another not so tense Super Sunday win, this time over the Denver Broncos by the score of 27–10. Precious as they may be to him, Roger the Dodger will not be remembered best for those lopsided Super Bowl wins. For in neither instance was he forced to do what he did better than anyone in NFL history up to that time: carve you up in the game's final minutes and filch victory.

Ask Minnesota. Staubach's 50-yard desperation heave to Drew Pearson—still known as the Hail Mary—with 24 seconds remaining in a '75 divisional playoff beat the Vikings, 17–14. Twenty-three times in his career, Staubach engineered fourth-quarter comebacks that led to victories; 14 of those came in overtime or the last two minutes of regulation.

While it was little consolation to him, Staubach provided much of the drama in Pittsburgh's Super Bowl defeats of his Cowboys, two of the best Super Sundays ever. With Pittsburgh up 21–10 in the fourth quarter of Supe X, Staubach hit Percy Howard—it was the only catch of his career—with a 34-yard scoring pass that brought the Cowboys to within striking distance. Staubach threw into the end zone on the game's final play.

Three Super Bowls later, the Cowboys trailed Pittsburgh 35–17 with 6:51 remaining when Staubach went to work. He took the team 89 yards in eight plays for one touchdown and—after defensive back Dennis Thurman pounced on the onside kick—52 yards in nine plays for another. Suddenly, it was 35–31.

That would be the final score but as they wrung their hands and swore on the sideline, the Steelers had no way of knowing it. "We had the game on ice, and now we're in trouble," moaned guard Gerry (Moon) Mullins. "Why do we always do this?"

That's an easy one, Moon. It's because you kept ending up in Super Bowls against Staubach.

Marcus **Allen**

He doesn't have great speed; he fumbles too often; he's the beneficiary of an excellent offensive line. These were the arguments critics of Marcus Allen made in 1982 against spending a high draft pick on the senior tailback out of Southern Cal. Even Allen's own coach seemed underwhelmed, despite the fact that Allen had rushed for 2,427 yards, 22 touchdowns and won the '81 Heisman Trophy. "I don't see him in the context of a Walter Payton or an Earl Campbell, a dominant player," said John Robinson.

Funny, Payton and Campbell were two of the Hall of Fame backs whose feats Allen would eclipse during a 16-year NFL career that saw him become the first player to surpass 10,000 yards rushing and 5,000 yards receiving. Allen's 123 career rushing touchdowns are an NFL record; his 12,243 rushing yards place him sixth on the alltime list. While Payton outrushed him, Allen boasts one trophy Sweetness lacks: the one given to the most valuable player in the Super Bowl.

Most NFL players finish their careers without getting a shot in the Big Game, so they know that given a chance in the Super Bowl, it's important to make the most of it. Allen reached just one Super Bowl in his 16 seasons, but did he ever make the most of it. The ex-Trojan joined the Raiders in '82, the same year their owner, Al Davis—having told his lawyers, "Just win, baby"—prevailed over the NFL in court and moved his team from Oakland to L.A. Up to that point, the Raiders had enjoyed success without a big-name running back, so it was a surprise when they made Allen the 10th pick of the '82 draft. Cynics suggested, and Davis denied, that drafting the local college star was a stunt to boost ticket sales in the L.A. Coliseum.

Allen immediately erased doubts that he would star on the pro level as well, rushing for 697 yards his first season and winning the NFL rookie-of-the-year award. He could run, catch, block and look after himself. During one Raider practice, Allen juked defensive tackle Lyle Alzado out of his jock, and received a shove in the back from Alzado after the play. Allen turned around and punched the veteran in the face.

In Allen's second pro season, the Raiders advanced to Super Bowl XVIII, where, it was widely believed, they would be masticated and expectorated by the defending champion Washington Redskins, who had won 11 straight games and 31 of their previous 34.

All Allen could muster against the league's top-rated run defense was 191 yards and two touchdowns on 20 carries. Late in the third quarter, Allen took the handoff, ran left, saw too much burgundy and commenced free-lancing. Reversing his field, he sliced through the middle of the Redskins defense and into the Super Bowl record books: His 74-yard touchdown run was the longest in the history of the game, and was the coup de grace, putting the Redskins in a 35–9 hole. The final score was 38–9; the AFC would not win another Super Bowl for 14 years.

Allen played nine more seasons for the Raiders, the final two marked by a rancorous, destructive feud with Davis, who traded him to Kansas City in '92. Allen, reborn in Kansas City, spent five productive seasons with the Chiefs before his retirement after the '97 season. When he is elected to the Hall of Fame—and he will be, though probably without Al Davis's vote—he has said that he will be enshrined as a Chief.

During Allen's final season, Chiefs head coach Marty Schottenheimer described him as the best short-yardage runner in NFL history. A fine compliment but Allen could not resist commenting, "There have been some long runs, too."

Timmy Smith (left) and Doug Williams

Timmy **Smith &**
Doug **Williams**

It was at once avuncular and R-rated. During a practice session five days before Super Bowl XXII in 1988, Doug Williams, the Washington Redskins' 32-year-old quarterback, read the riot act to rookie running back Timmy Smith, who had just fumbled twice during the same drill.

"I've been trying to get to this [game] for 11 years," shouted Williams, "and I'm not going to let you screw it up. If you fumble that [ball] on Sunday, I'll personally kick your ass."

Williams could be excused for being a little cranky, having spent the better part of the week fielding variations of the same question: *How does it feel to be the first black quarterback to start in a Super Bowl?*

It hurts like hell. That's how Williams might have responded late in the first quarter, when he twisted— "hyperflexed" was the official diagnosis—his left knee. Walking back to the huddle, he collapsed.

After missing one series, Williams re-entered the game and called a fly pattern to wideout Ricky Sanders on a quick count. Sanders stutter-stepped, then blew past Denver Broncos cornerback Mark Haynes for an 80-yard score. The Golden Quarter, as Redskins fans refer to it, had begun. Williams's second TD pass, to receiver Gary Clark, went for 27 yards. Two series later Sanders latched onto another scoring pass, this one a 50-yarder. An eight-yard catch by tight end Clint Didier capped the most prolific period in Super Bowl history: 356 yards of total offense and five touchdowns on five possessions.

One of those touchdowns came on the ground. Smith,

a fifth-round pick out of Texas Tech who had gained only 126 yards during the regular season, had earned the start in Supe XXII by ratcheting up his intensity in the playoffs. The rookie was not informed that he would be starting until just before kickoff. "We didn't want him vomiting in the locker room," one Skins coach explained.

Smith took the news calmly. When Williams called "Counter Gap, right," during the Redskins third series of the second quarter, Smith took the handoff, settled in behind pulling linemen Raleigh McKenzie and Joe Jacoby and did not stop until he reached the end zone. That 58-yard run put the Redskins up 21–10 and was the highlight of Smith's sensational day: 204 yards and two touchdowns on 22 carries.

The 204-yard rushing performance stands as a Super Bowl record, and would have earned Smith the MVP award in any other NFL title game. As it happened, the guy handing the ball to him was having a historic day. Playing on a creaking knee and under a media microscope, Williams threw for 340 yards and four touchdowns. He spent the days before the game reminding reporters that he was Washington's quarterback, not the black quarterback. Still, Williams understood the significance of his start. Years later, he would often ask himself, *What if I'd been a failure?*

He was anything but, and Williams can live happily with the knowledge that in one of the most pressure-packed moments in sports history, he did not stumble.

And Smith did not fumble.

Troy **Aikman**

Barry Switzer was about to introduce himself to Troy Aikman when someone threw Aikman a football. They were on a practice field at Oklahoma, where Switzer was the head football coach and Aikman was a gangly teenager turning a lot of heads at a football camp. Aikman threw the ball back, and Switzer said to himself, *This kid is different.*

"I watched him throw it five or six times," recalled Switzer. "Then I offered him a scholarship on the spot."

Aikman eventually accepted that offer. After two years, however—this would emerge as a pattern in his life—Aikman became unhappy in Switzer's program. He transferred to UCLA, where he led the Bruins to a 20–4 record over two years. In the 1989 draft he was the No. 1 overall pick. He was selected by the Dallas Cowboys, whom he would lead to three Super Bowls in four years.

To get to that heavenly plateau, Aikman went through hell. As a rookie, he went 0–11 and missed five games with a broken finger. After throwing a go-ahead touchdown pass against the Phoenix Cardinals late in the 14th game of the year, Aikman was knocked unconscious, then helped from the field with blood dripping from his ear. Aikman says he was so thrashed after that 1–15 season, "I had no idea how some of my teammates had played 10 years in the NFL." At the time, he recalls, "there was nothing fun about football."

But fun was just around the corner. In the '92 playoffs Aikman completed 61 of 89 passes—with eight touchdowns and no interceptions—for 795 yards. His quarterback rating was a stratospheric 126.4. He threw four touchdown passes in the Cowboys' 35-point win over the Buffalo Bills in Super Bowl XXVII and won the MVP award.

It was during Dallas's reign atop the NFL—the Cowboys rolled over Buffalo in Supe XXVIII too as Aikman completed 70.4 percent of his passes—that he became a prisoner of his own fame. Aikman went clothes shopping by asking stores to remain open after hours; did his grocery shopping by e-mail. It was, Aikman admitted, a high price for success. His dissatisfaction was compounded by the departure of his friend and coach Jimmy Johnson, who feuded with Jones and left, to be replaced by Switzer. Dallas won the Super Bowl in Switzer's second season. While Aikman was solid in that 27–17 victory over the Steelers, hitting 10 straight passes at one point, the Cowboys owed their Supe XXX victory to Pittsburgh quarterback Neil O'Donnell, who threw two critical interceptions to Dallas cornerback Larry Brown.

After the game, a jubilant Switzer shouted to his team, "Let's win the party!" Sadly, the Cowboys took him literally. If it wasn't wide receiver Michael Irvin pleading no contest to a felony cocaine possession charge, it was offensive tackle Erik Williams nearly killing himself in a car wreck, or defensive tackle Leon Lett flunking his second drug test. Aikman, who missed the tight ship run by Johnson, was not exactly broken up by Switzer's resignation after the '97 season.

New coach Chan Gailey vowed to impose more structure on the team, but can he reverse the crumbling of a dynasty? Stranger things have happened. As the '98 season approached, tub-of-goo guard Nate Newton had lost 60 pounds, and Irvin had, uh, kept his nose clean.

And the perpetually tormented Aikman was actually in a great mood, talking about playing "another four, five, even six" years. A happy Aikman could do a lot for Dallas's quest to return to the Super Bowl. As an old coach of his once said, this kid is different.

R i c h a r d **Dent**

He began the game on his back, looking up at the lights of the Louisiana Superdome and hoping no one would step on him. The most valuable player of Super Bowl XX was, on his first play of the day, its most vulnerable. Chicago Bears defensive end Richard Dent had been waiting for a run, but the New England Patriots passed. Or so Dent was later informed. Patriots offensive tackle Brian Holloway caught him looking and knocked him ass-over-bandbox.

"I had never been hit like that before," said Dent, who nonetheless saw some good in his temporary humiliation. "The first lick is what you need. It gets you going."

Holloway's pancake block awakened a giant. On New England's second series, Dent and linebacker Wilber Marshall shared a 10-yard sack of quarterback Tony Eason that forced a punt. On the second play of the Patriots' third series, Eason dropped back to pass and was stripped by Dent; defensive tackle Dan Hampton recovered the ball on New England's 13-yard line. The Bears got a field goal out of it. After the kickoff Patriots running back Craig James swept left and was stripped—forgive us if this is getting monotonous—by Dent; linebacker Mike Singletary picked up the ball on New England's 13-yard-line. Largely due to the ubiquitous Dent, Da Bears led 13–3 at the end of the first quarter, and for all practical purposes, the game was over. It seemed overwhelmingly clear after the Patriots' second series that the only direction they would move the ball against this Bears defense was backwards. Indeed, New England finished the first half in the red for total offense, with minus-19 yards.

The final score was 46–10, and it could have been worse. New England's offensive linemen were overmatched by Chicago's seven-man rush, although Eason could have been forgiven for thinking that the Bears were sending only one guy, No. 95. Dent had rebounded with a vengeance after Holloway had deposited him on his butt.

Make that his skinny butt. At a scouting combine before the 1983 draft, Philadelphia Eagles head coach Marion Campbell was taken into the locker room by a scout. There was Dent, naked, with his back turned.

"Too skinny," said Campbell. "I don't want anyone with a skinny rear end like that."

Nice instincts, Marion.

But it's unfair to single out Campbell for whiffing on Dent: 202 selections were made before the Bears took the 6' 3½", 224-pound end out of Tennessee State in the eighth round. The credit for eventually making the selection goes to the Bears' personnel director, Bill Tobin, who after watching Dent on film wrote, "This kid gets a zero for quickness off the ball." Scouting grades are like golf scores, the lower the better. Dent had some quicks. And guts. During his senior season, he broke his arm but continued to play, eventually with a plate inserted to protect it. The injury depressed his stock, as did Tobin's assessment at the scouting combine: "I'm embarrassed for the way his body looks. Flat feet. Very poor body for defensive end."

On draft day the Bears had other things to be embarrassed about. Dent was still there in the fourth round of the draft, but Chicago selected guard Tom Thayer instead, only to discover that Thayer had signed with the USFL two hours earlier. And the Bears had traded their fifth, sixth and seventh round picks.

Miraculously, Dent was still available in the eighth round. Chicago took him, broken arm, flat feet, skinny behind and all. Dent kept growing—he was listed at 6'5", 270 pounds for most of his career—and overcame his myriad perceived physical shortcomings to rack up 402 tackles, 141.5 sacks and one Super Bowl MVP over the next 15 seasons.

FOURTH QUARTER:

the game in pictures

FOURTH QUARTER

The Game in Pictures

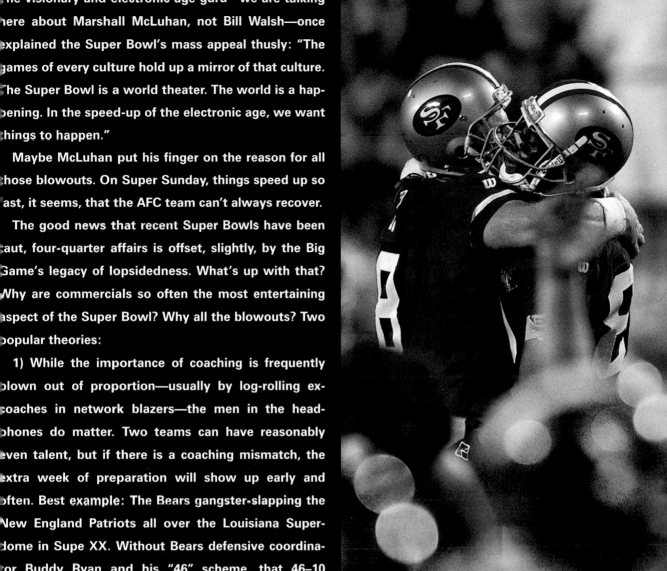

The visionary and electronic age guru—we are talking here about Marshall McLuhan, not Bill Walsh—once explained the Super Bowl's mass appeal thusly: "The games of every culture hold up a mirror of that culture. The Super Bowl is a world theater. The world is a happening. In the speed-up of the electronic age, we want things to happen."

Maybe McLuhan put his finger on the reason for all those blowouts. On Super Sunday, things speed up so fast, it seems, that the AFC team can't always recover.

The good news that recent Super Bowls have been taut, four-quarter affairs is offset, slightly, by the Big Game's legacy of lopsidedness. What's up with that? Why are commercials so often the most entertaining aspect of the Super Bowl? Why all the blowouts? Two popular theories:

1) While the importance of coaching is frequently blown out of proportion—usually by log-rolling ex-coaches in network blazers—the men in the head-phones do matter. Two teams can have reasonably even talent, but if there is a coaching mismatch, the extra week of preparation will show up early and often. Best example: The Bears gangster-slapping the New England Patriots all over the Louisiana Super-dome in Supe XX. Without Bears defensive coordina-tor Buddy Ryan and his "46" scheme, that 46–10 blowout might have been a game.

2) Being humans rather than cyborgs (again, with the possible exception of Joe Montana), the players feel the pressure. Every play, every potential momen-tum swing, is magnified and assumes a Super signifi-cance. Ripples turn into tidal waves. Thus does Jim Kelly's first-quarter interception to Dallas Cowboys safety James Washington become the first of a Super Bowl–record nine turnovers by the Buffalo Bills in their 52–17 Supe XXVII loss. The team that is not careful can take on a deer-in-the-headlights look before the first quarter is over, as did the San Diego Chargers in Super Bowl XXIX, when the 49ers scored on their first two possessions en route to a 49–26 slaughter.

In the pages that follow we present a picture act of

The Bears defense (opposite) would have been a lot less fearsome without Ryan's brilliant "46" scheme; San Francisco's Steve Young (above right) and Jerry Rice made the most of San Diego's deer-in-the-headlights paralysis, connect-ing on three TD passes in the Supe XXIX rout

images from games we have not chosen to revisit elsewhere. Just because the drama has been drained from a Super Bowl before the halftime antics of our ever-engaging friends at Up With People (speaking of cyborgs); just because a game lacks suspense, does not mean it must lack memorable moments. Turn the page, and see for yourself.

Jim O'Brien kicks the winning 32-yard field goal in the closing seconds of blunder-filled Super Bowl V, a 16–13 Colts victory over the Cowboys that featured a combined six fumbles, six interceptions, a muffed field goal attempt and a blocked PAT.

The Miami Dolphins took a 17–10 halftime lead in Super Bowl XVII after
Fulton Walker (above) ran 98 yards to score the first touchdown on a kickoff
return in Super Bowl history. But in the second half Miami would be limited to
two first downs and zero points as Washington rallied to win, 27-17.

San Francisco's Eric Wright picked off a third-quarter pass intended for Miami's Mark Clayton (right) as the 49ers rolled over the Dolphins in Super Bowl XIX, 38-16.

Facing wild-card Oakland in Super Bowl XV, Philadelphia's Ron Jaworski had a wild day himself: He threw one of his three inteceptions on his first attempt; had a 40-yard touchdown pass to Rodney Parker wiped out by a penalty; fumbled away a snap; and completed just 18 of 38 passes. The end result—Oakland 27, Philadelphia 10.

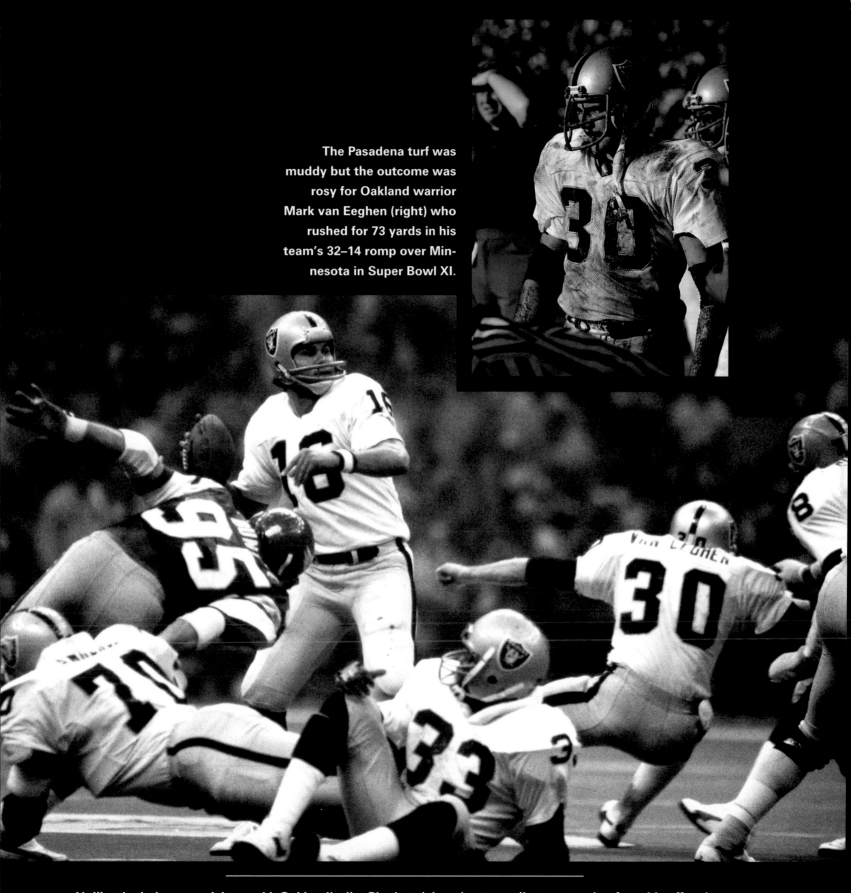

The Pasadena turf was muddy but the outcome was rosy for Oakland warrior Mark van Eeghen (right) who rushed for 73 yards in his team's 32–14 romp over Minnesota in Super Bowl XI.

Unlike the beleaguered Jaworski, Oakland's Jim Plunkett (above) got excellent protection from his offensive line, being sacked just once while completing 61.9% of his passes for 261 yards, three touchdowns and no interceptions; for his performance, Plunkett took home the game's MVP award.

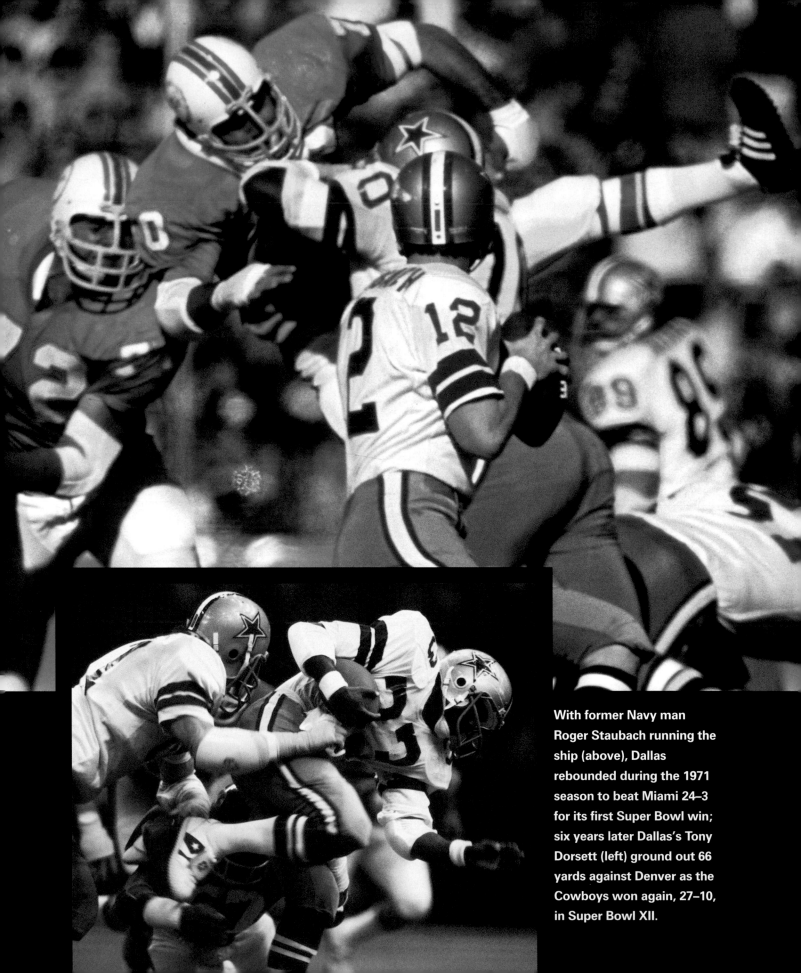

With former Navy man Roger Staubach running the ship (above), Dallas rebounded during the 1971 season to beat Miami 24–3 for its first Super Bowl win; six years later Dallas's Tony Dorsett (left) ground out 66 yards against Denver as the Cowboys won again, 27–10, in Super Bowl XII.

Washington's John Riggins (above), often festooned with would-be Miami tacklers, carried the ball 38 times for 166 yards in the Redskins' 27–17 Super Bowl XVII victory. The key play was Riggo's 43-yard touchdown gallop on fourth-and-inches that put the Redskins ahead, 20–17, in the fourth quarter.

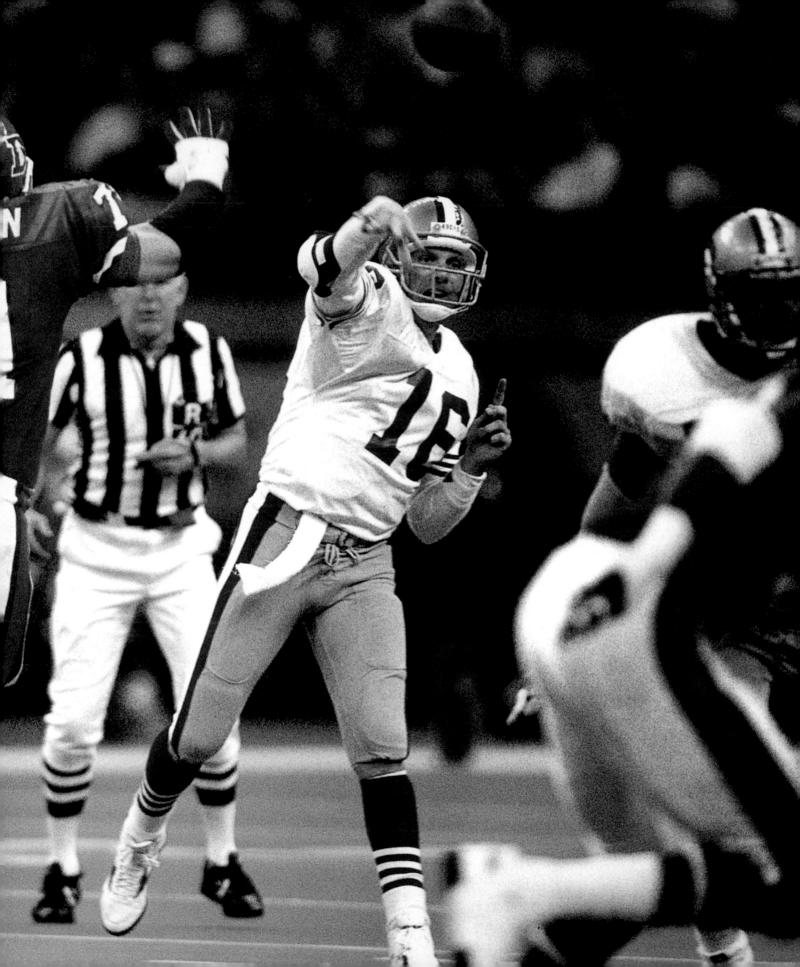

Pity the lowly Broncos, who fell thuddingly four times before their sentinmental win
in Supe XXXII; among their nemeses were San Francisco and Joe Montana (left),
who decimated them on 22-for-29 passing for 297 yards and a record five TDS in a 55–10
Super Bowl XXIV drubbing, and the Giants and their fearsome defense, led by
Lawrence Taylor (56), Jim Burt (64) and Carl Banks (58), which hounded the Denver offense
into an interception, four sacks and a safety in New York's 39–20 Super Bowl XXI win.

The cerebral Bob Griese (above) capped Miami's perfect 1972 season by producing just enough offense to keep the Dolphins' winning streak intact with a narrow 14–7 victory over Washington in Super Bowl VII; a pair of interceptions by Thomas Everett (right) was just one factor in Dallas's 52–17 demolition of the Bills in Super Bowl XXVII; Troy Aikman's performance, including 273 passing yards for four touchdowns, was another

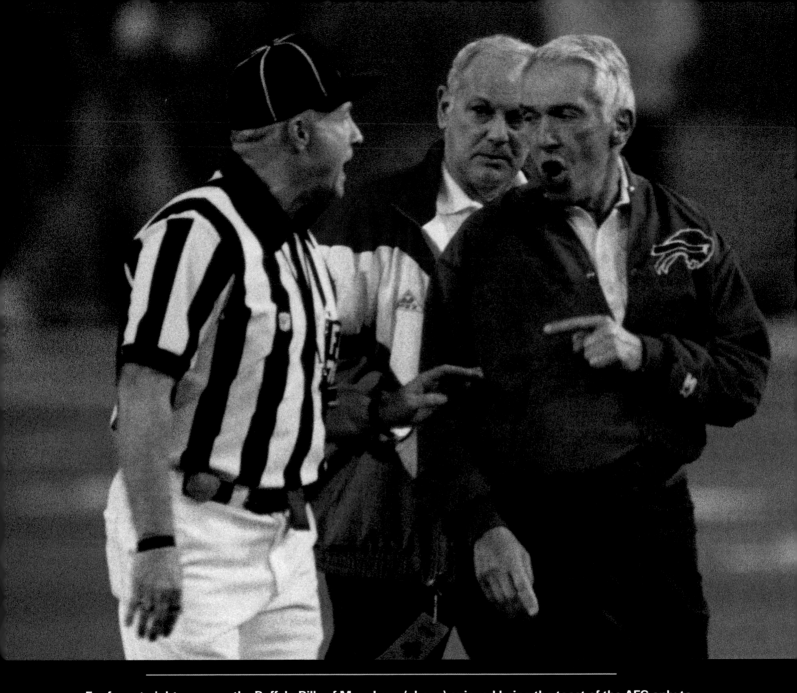

For four straight seasons, the Buffalo Bills of Marv Levy (above) enjoyed being the toast of the AFC only to taste bitter defeat on Super Bowl Sunday. After losing a nailbiter to New York in Super Bowl XXV due to Scott Norwood's wide-right field-goal attempt, the next three title games were marked by costly turnovers and larger losing margins as the Bills fell by 13, 35 and 17 points in Super Bowls XXVI, XXVII and XXVIII respectively.

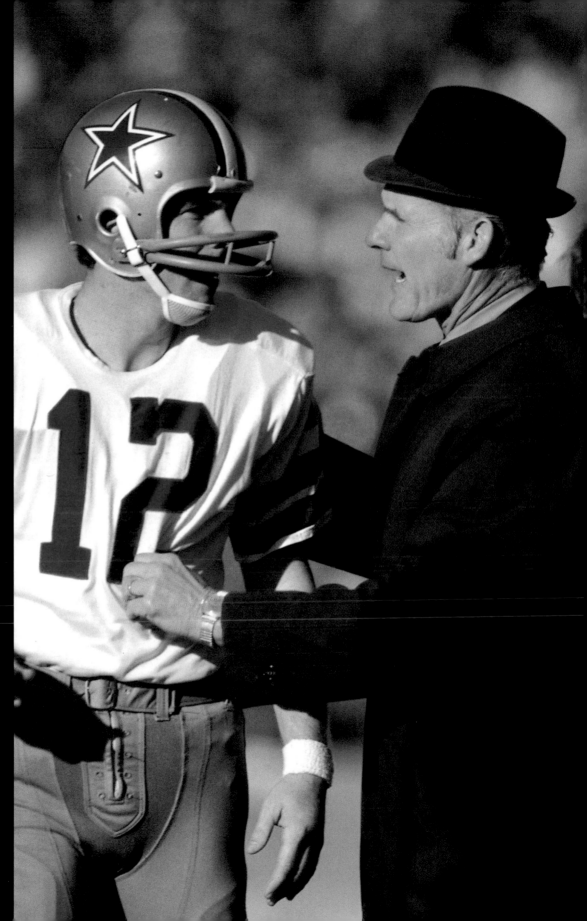

Unable to win Super Bowl V with Craig Morton at the helm, Tom Landry inserted Roger Staubach midway through the 1971 season, and the Cowboys won the next ten games, including Supe VI

With Darryl Johnston (left) and the Cowboys' running game quieted to a mere whisper in the second half of Dallas's Super Bowl XXX matchup against Pittsburgh, America's Team needed a pair of interceptions by MVP Larry Brown to produce the 14 points thatput the game out of reach en route to a 27–17 final score.

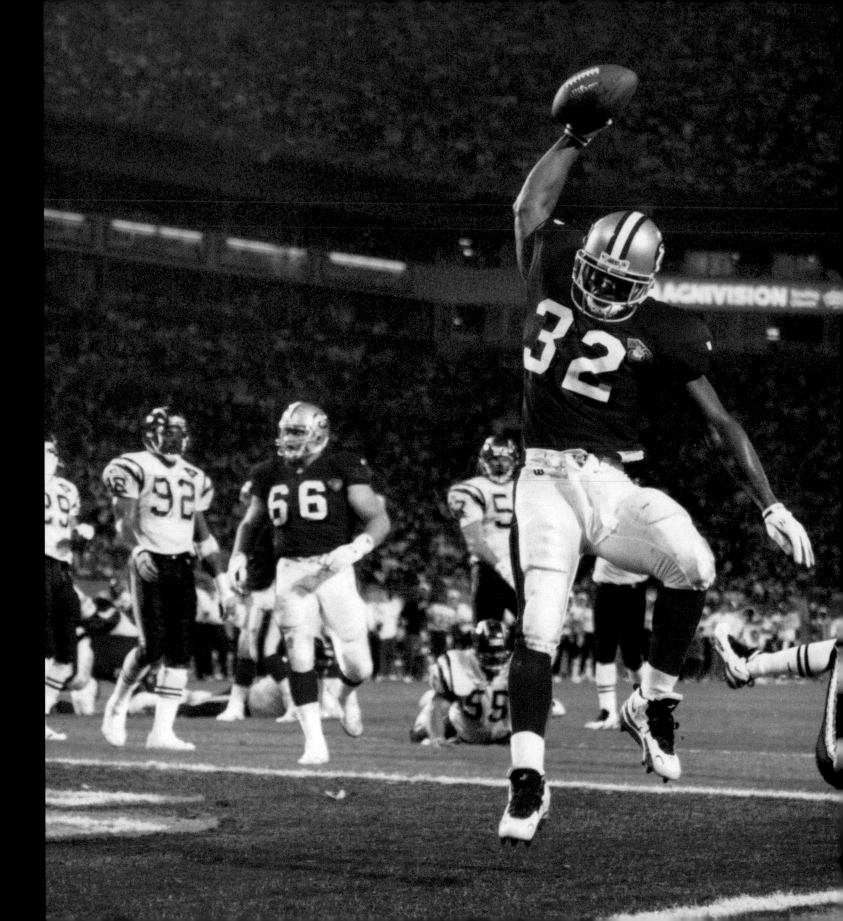

9:36   Marlboro   Marlboro

Ricky Watters's jubilant spike (left) after his eight-yard touchdown catch put the 49ers up 28–7 in Super Bowl XXIX pretty well summed up the day for San Francisco; Watters and wide receiver Jerry Rice had three touchdowns apiece in the 49-26 thrashing of San Diego while MVP Steve Young threw a record six touchdown passes and was also the game's leading rusher with 49 yards on five carries.

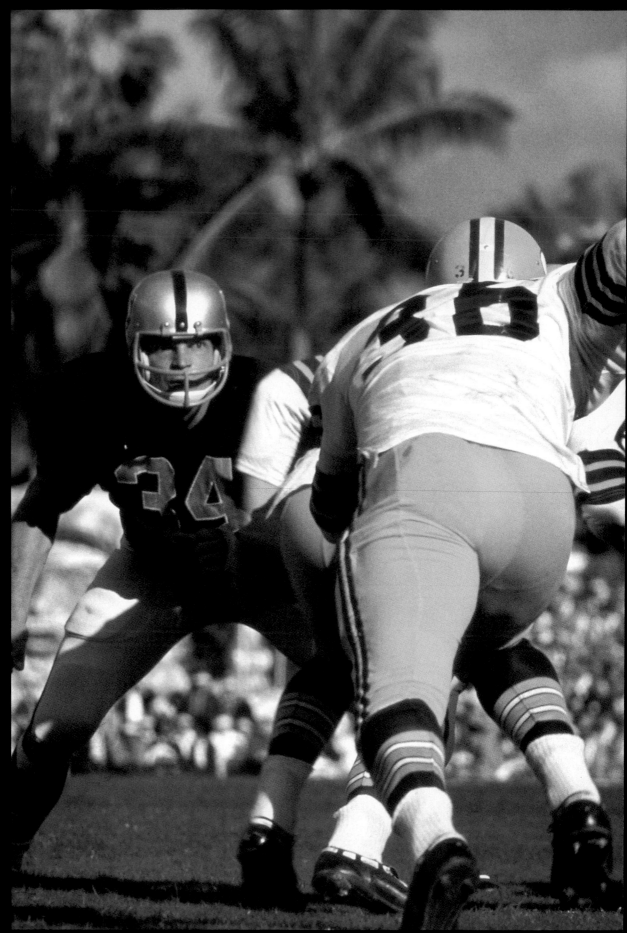

Just fourteen days but seemingly a world away from the –13° temperatures they endured to win the "ice bowl" and the NFL championship over Dallas, Bart Starr (right) and the Green Bay Packers nonetheless seemed right at home in tropical Miami, rolling to an easy 33–14 defeat of the AFL champion Oakland Raiders in Super Bowl II. Starr's numbers: 202 passing yards, one touchdown, no interceptions.

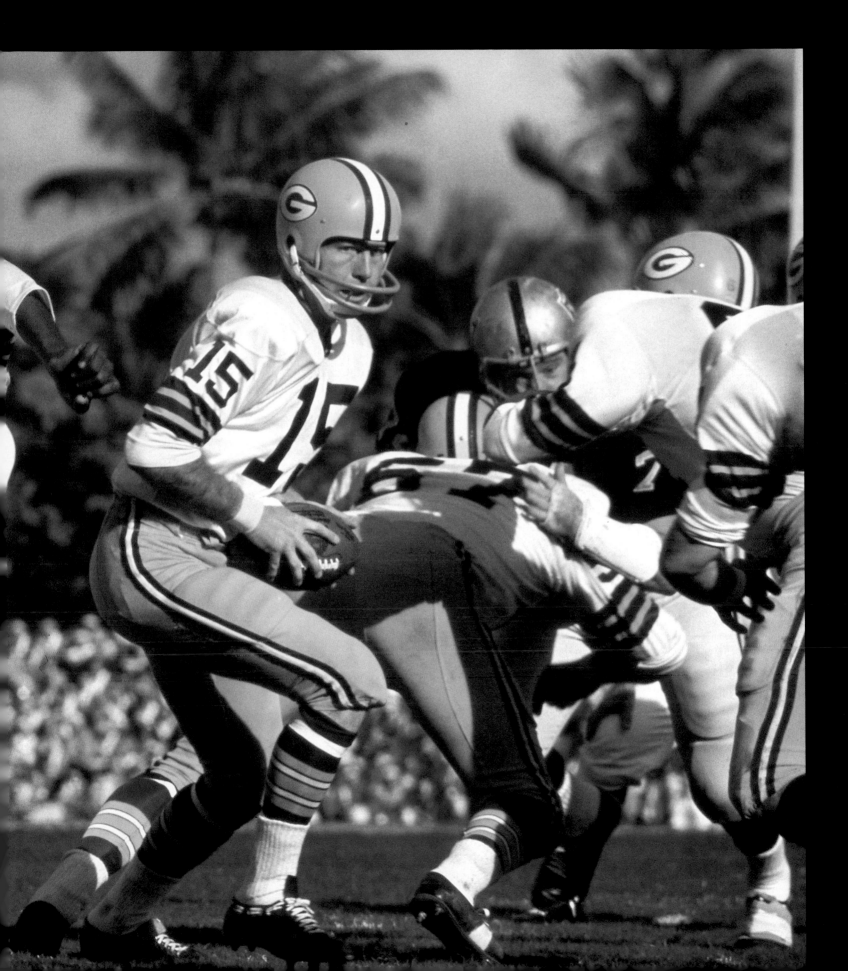

It was a bittersweet embrace after Super Bowl XXVIII, sweet for Dallas's Emmitt Smith, but bitter for Buffalo's Thurman Thomas, whose brilliance in the regular season could not make up for his team's abysmal performance against the Cowboys, who thrashed the Bills in back-to-back Bowls by a combined score of 82–30.

It was a Chicago fire at the Superdome in New Orleans as the Bears' aggressive defense torched the New England Patriots for seven sacks and limited them to seven rushing yards in Super Bowl XX. The Dogs also scored eight points in the 46–10 rout on a safety and an interception return by Reggie Phillips (left).

The Super Bowl

r e s u l t s

	Date	Winner (Share)	Loser (Share)	Score	Site (Attendance)
I	1-15-67	Green Bay ($15,000)	Kansas City ($7,500)	35–10	Los Angeles (61,946)
II	1-14-68	Green Bay ($15,000)	Oakland ($7,500)	33–14	Miami (75,546)
III	1-12-69	NY Jets ($15,000)	Baltimore ($7,500)	16–7	Miami (75,389)
IV	1-11-70	Kansas City ($15,000)	Minnesota ($7,500)	23–7	New Orleans (80,562)
V	1-17-71	Baltimore ($15,000)	Dallas ($7,500)	16–13	Miami (79,204)
VI	1-16-72	Dallas ($15,000)	Miami ($7,500)	24–3	New Orleans (81,023)
VII	1-14-73	Miami ($15,000)	Washington ($7,500)	14–7	Los Angeles (90,182)
VIII	1-13-74	Miami ($15,000)	Minnesota ($7,500)	24–7	Houston (71,882)
IX	1-12-75	Pittsburgh ($15,000)	Minnesota ($7,500)	16–6	New Orleans (80,997)
X	1-18-76	Pittsburgh ($15,000)	Dallas ($7,500)	21–17	Miami (80,187)
XI	1-9-77	Oakland ($15,000)	Minnesota ($7,500)	32–14	Pasadena (103,438)
XII	1-15-78	Dallas ($18,000)	Denver ($9,000)	27–10	New Orleans (75,583)
XIII	1-21-79	Pittsburgh ($18,000)	Dallas ($9,000)	35–31	Miami (79,484)
XIV	1-20-80	Pittsburgh ($18,000)	Los Angeles ($9,000)	31–19	Pasadena (103,985)
XV	1-25-81	Oakland ($18,000)	Philadelphia ($9,000)	27–10	New Orleans (76,135)
XVI	1-24-82	San Francisco ($18,000)	Cincinnati ($9,000)	26–21	Pontiac, Mich. (81,270)
XVII	1-30-83	Washington ($36,000)	Miami ($18,000)	27–17	Pasadena (103,667)
XVIII	1-22-84	LA Raiders ($36,000)	Washington ($18,000)	38–9	Tampa (72,920)
XIX	1-20-85	San Francisco ($36,000)	Miami ($18,000)	38–16	Stanford (84,059)
XX	1-26-86	Chicago ($36,000)	New England ($18,000)	46–10	New Orleans (73,818)
XXI	1-25-87	NY Giants ($36,000)	Denver ($18,000)	39–20	Pasadena (101,063)
XXII	1-31-88	Washington ($36,000)	Denver ($18,000)	42–10	San Diego (73,302)
XXIII	1-22-89	San Francisco ($36,000)	Cincinnati ($18,000)	20–16	Miami (75,129)
XXIV	1-28-90	San Francisco ($36,000)	Denver ($18,000)	55–10	New Orleans (72,919)
XXV	1-27-91	NY Giants ($36,000)	Buffalo ($18,000)	20–19	Tampa (73,813)
XXVI	1-26-92	Washington ($36,000)	Buffalo ($18,000)	37–24	Minneapolis (63,130)
XXVII	1-31-93	Dallas ($36,000)	Buffalo ($18,000)	52–17	Pasadena (98,374)
XXVIII	1-30-94	Dallas ($38,000)	Buffalo ($23,500)	30–13	Atlanta (72,817)
XXIX	1-29-95	San Francisco ($42,000)	San Diego ($26,000)	49–26	Miami (74,107)
XXX	1-28-96	Dallas ($42,000)	Pittsburgh ($27,000)	27–17	Tempe, Ariz. (76,347)
XXXI	1-26-97	Green Bay ($48,000)	New England ($29,000)	35–21	New Orleans (72,301)
XXXII	1-25-98	Denver ($48,000)	Green Bay ($27,500)	31–24	San Diego (68,912)

m o s t   v a l u a b l e   p l a y e r s

	Player	Team	Position	Key Statistics
I	Bart Starr	GB	QB	16-for-23 passing, 250 yards, two TDs.
II	Bart Starr	GB	QB	13-for-24 passing, 202 yards, one TD, no INTs.
III	Joe Namath	NYJ	QB	17-for-28 passing, 206 yards, no INTs.
IV	Len Dawson	KC	QB	12-for-17 passing, 142 yards.
V	Chuck Howley	Dall	LB	Two INTs, including one in the Dallas end zone.
VI	Roger Staubach	Dall	QB	12-for-19 passing, 119 yards, two TDs, no INTs.
VII	Jake Scott	Mia	S	Two INTs, one returned 55 yards from the Miami end zone.
VIII	Larry Csonka	Mia	RB	33 carries for 145 rushing yards, two TDs.
IX	Franco Harris	Pitt	RB	34 carries for 158 rushing yards, one TD.
X	Lynn Swann	Pitt	WR	4 catches for 161 yards, one TD.
XI	Fred Biletnikoff	Oak	WR	4 catches for 79 yards, 48-yarder to set up TD.

most valuable players

	Player	Team	Position	Key Statistics
XII	Randy White	Dall	DT	Five tackles, one assist.
	Harvey Martin	Dall	DE	Two tackles, two sacks, one deflection.
XIII	Terry Bradshaw	Pitt	QB	17-for-30 passing, 318 yards, four TDs.
XIV	Terry Bradshaw	Pitt	QB	14-for-21 passing, 309 yards, two TDs.
XV	Jim Plunkett	Oak	QB	13-for-21 passing, 261 yards, three TDs, no INTs.
XVI	Joe Montana	SF	QB	14-for-24 passing, 157 yards, one TD, one rushing TD.
XVII	John Riggins	Wash	RB	38 carries for 166 rushing yards, one TD.
XVIII	Marcus Allen	LARai	RB	20 carries for 191 rushing yards, two TDs.
XIX	Joe Montana	SF	QB	24-for-35 passing, 331 yards, three TDs, one rushing TD.
XX	Richard Dent	Chi	DE	Two sacks, two forced fumbles.
XXI	Phil Simms	NYG	QB	22-for-25 passing, 268 yards, three TDs, no INTs.
XXII	Doug Williams	Wash	QB	18-for-29 passing, 340 yards, four TDs.
XXIII	Jerry Rice	SF	WR	11 catches for 215 yards, one TD.
XXIV	Joe Montana	SF	QB	22-for-29 passing, 297 yards, four TDs, no INTs.
XXV	Ottis Anderson	NYG	RB	21 carries for 102 rushing yards, one TD.
XXVI	Mark Rypien	Wash	QB	18-for-33 passing, 292 yards, two TDs.
XXVII	Troy Aikman	Dall	QB	22-for-30 passing, 273 yards, four TDs, no INTs.
XXVIII	Emmitt Smith	Dall	RB	30 carries for 132 rushing yards, two TDs.
XXIX	Steve Young	SF	QB	24-for-36 passing, 325 yards, six TDs.
XXX	Larry Brown	Dall	DB	Two INTs that set up TDs.
XXXI	Desmond Howard	GB	KR	99-yard kickoff return for TD, 244 total return yards.
XXXII	Terrell Davis	Den	RB	30 carries for 157 rushing yards, three TDs.

composite standings

	W	L	Pct	Pts	Opp Pts
San Francisco 49ers	5	0	1.000	188	89
NY Giants	2	0	1.000	59	39
Chicago Bears	1	0	1.000	46	10
NY Jets	1	0	1.000	16	7
Pittsburgh Steelers	4	1	.800	120	100
Green Bay Packers	3	1	.750	127	76
Oakland/LA Raiders	3	1	.750	111	66
Dallas Cowboys	5	3	.625	221	132
Washington Redskins	3	2	.600	122	103
Baltimore Colts	1	1	.500	23	29
Kansas City Chiefs	1	1	.500	33	42
Miami Dolphins	2	3	.400	74	103
Denver Broncos	1	4	.200	81	187
LA Rams	0	1	.000	19	31
Philadelphia Eagles	0	1	.000	10	27
San Diego Chargers	0	1	.000	26	49
Cincinnati Bengals	0	2	.000	37	46
New England Patriots	0	2	.000	31	81
Buffalo Bills	0	4	.000	73	139
Minnesota Vikings	0	4	.000	34	95

Career Leaders

passing

	GP	Att	Comp Pct	Comp	Yds	Avg Gain	TD	Pct TD	Int	Pct Int	Lg	Passer Rating
Joe Montana, SF	4	122	83	68.0	1142	9.36	11	9.0	0	0.0	44	127.8
Jim Plunkett, Rai	2	46	29	63.0	433	9.41	4	8.7	0	0.0	t80	122.8
Terry Bradshaw, Pitt	4	84	49	58.3	932	11.10	9	10.7	4	4.8	t75	112.8
Troy Aikman, Dall	3	80	56	70.0	689	8.61	5	6.3	1	1.3	t56	111.9
Bart Starr, GB	2	47	29	61.7	452	9.62	3	6.4	1	2.1	t62	106.0
Brett Favre, GB	2	69	39	56.5	502	7.28	5	7.2	1	1.4	t81	97.7
Roger Staubach, Dall	4	98	61	62.2	734	7.49	8	8.2	4	4.1	t45	95.4
Len Dawson, KC	2	44	28	63.6	353	8.02	2	4.5	2	4.5	t46	84.8
Bob Griese, Mia	3	41	26	63.4	295	7.20	1	2.4	2	4.9	t28	72.7
Dan Marino, Mia	1	50	29	58.0	318	6.36	1	2.0	2	4.0	30	66.9

Note: Minimum 40 attempts.

rushing

	GP	Yds	Att	Avg	Lg	TD
Franco Harris, Pitt	4	354	101	3.5	25	4
Larry Csonka, Mia	3	297	57	5.2	9	2
Emmitt Smith, Dall	3	289	70	4.1	38	5
John Riggins, Wash	2	230	64	3.6	43	2
Timmy Smith, Wash	1	204	22	9.3	58	2
Thurman Thomas, Buff	4	204	52	3.9	31	4
Roger Craig, SF	3	198	52	3.8	18	2
Marcus Allen, Rai	1	191	20	9.6	t74	2
Tony Dorsett, Dall	2	162	31	5.2	29	1
Terrell Davis, Den	1	157	30	5.2	27	3

receiving

	GP	No.	Yds	Avg	Lg	TD
Jerry Rice, SF	3	28	512	18.3	t44	7
Andre Reed, Buff	4	27	323	11.9	40	0
Roger Craig, SF	3	20	212	10.6	40	2
Thurman Thomas, Buff	4	20	144	7.2	24	0
Tom Novacek, Dall	3	17	178	10.5	23	2
Lynn Swann, Pitt	4	16	364	22.8	t64	3
Michael Irvin, Dall	3	16	256	16.0	25	2
Chuck Foreman, Minn	3	15	139	9.3	26	0
Cliff Branch, Rai	3	14	181	12.9	50	3
Preston Pearson, Balt-Pitt-Dall	5	12	105	8.8	14	0
Don Beebe, Buff-GB	5	12	171	14.3	43	2
Kenneth Davis, Buff	4	12	72	6.0	19	0
Antonio Freeman, GB	2	12	231	19.3	t81	3

Single-Game Leaders

scoring

	Pts
Roger Craig:	
XIX, San Francisco vs Miami (1 R, 2 P)	18
Jerry Rice:	
XXIV, San Francisco vs Denver (3 P);	
XXIX, SF vs San Diego (3 P)	18
Ricky Watters:	
XXIX, San Francisco vs San Diego (1 R, 2 P)	18
Terrell Davis:	
XXXII, Denver vs Green Bay (3 R)	18

rushing yards

	Yds
Timmy Smith: XXII, Washington vs Denver	204
Marcus Allen: XVIII, LA Raiders vs Washington	191
John Riggins: XVII, Washington vs Miami	166
Franco Harris: IX, Pittsburgh vs Minnesota	158
Terrell Davis: XXXII, Denver vs Green Bay	157
Larry Csonka: VIII, Miami vs Minnesota	145
Clarence Davis: XI, Oakland vs Minnesota	137
Thurman Thomas: XXV, Buffalo vs NY Giants	135
Emmitt Smith: XXVIII, Dallas vs Buffalo	132
Matt Snell: III, NY Jets vs Baltimore Colts	121

receptions

	No.
Dan Ross: XVI, Cincinnati vs San Francisco	11
Jerry Rice: XXIII, San Francisco vs Cincinnati	11
Tony Nathan: XIX, Miami vs San Francisco	10
Jerry Rice: XXIX, San Francisco vs San Diego	10
Andre Hastings: XXX, Pittsburgh vs Dallas	10
Ricky Sanders: XXII, Washington vs Denver	9
Antonio Freeman: XXXII, Green Bay vs Denver	9

Six tied with 8.

touchdown passes

	No.
Steve Young: XXIX, San Francisco vs San Diego	6
Joe Montana: XXIV, San Francisco vs Denver	5
Terry Bradshaw: XIII, Pittsburgh vs Dallas	4
Doug Williams: XXII, Washington vs Denver	4
Troy Aikman: XXVII, Dallas vs Buffalo	4

Five tied with 3.

receiving yards

	Yds
Jerry Rice: XXIII, San Francisco vs Cincinnati	215
Ricky Sanders: XXII, Washington vs Denver	193
Lynn Swann: X, Pittsburgh vs Dallas	161
Andre Reed: XXVII, Buffalo vs Dallas	152
Jerry Rice: XXIX, San Francisco vs San Diego	149
Jerry Rice: XXIV, San Francisco vs Denver	148
Max McGee: I, Green Bay vs Kansas City	138
George Sauer: III, NY Jets vs Baltimore	133

passing yards

	Yds
Joe Montana: XXIII, San Francisco vs Cincinnati	357
Doug Williams: XXII, Washington vs Denver	340
Joe Montana: XIX, San Francisco vs Miami	331
Steve Young: XXIX, San Francisco vs San Diego	325
Terry Bradshaw: XIII, Pittsburgh vs Dallas	318
Dan Marino: XIX, Miami vs San Francisco	318
Terry Bradshaw: XIV, Pittsburgh vs LA Rams	309
John Elway: XXI, Denver vs NY Giants	304

Photography Credits

Front Cover, Neil Leifer; **back cover**, Robert Beck.

Front Matter
Half-title page, Tony Triolo; Title page, James Drake.

Introduction
6, John Iacono; 8, Jerry Wachter; 9, John Iacono; 10, Walter Iooss Jr.; 11, John Iacono.

First Quarter: The Games
12-13, Neil Leifer; 14, Neil Leifer; 16, Richard Mackson; 17, Walter Iooss Jr.; 18, Damian Strohmeyer; 20, Damian Strohmeyer; 21, Heinz Kluetmeier; 23, Walter Iooss Jr.; 24, Damian Strohmeyer; 25, Walter Iooss Jr.; 27, John Biever; 28, Heinz Kluetmeier; 28-29, John McDonough; 30, Herb Scharfman; 32, Walter Iooss Jr.; 32-33, Neil Leifer; 33, Walter Iooss Jr.; 35, Al Tielemans; 36, Al Tielemans; 37, Damian Strohmeyer; 38, Heinz Kluetmeier; 40, Neil Leifer; 41, Walter Iooss Jr.; 42, Neil Leifer; 44, Walter Iooss Jr.; 45, Neil Leifer; 47, Heinz Kluetmeier; 48 top, Tony Tomsic; bottom, Tony Tomsic; 49, James Drake; 51, Walter Iooss Jr.; 52, Walter Iooss Jr.; 53, Walter Iooss Jr.; 54, Walter Iooss Jr.; 56, Walter Iooss Jr.; 57, John Iacono.

Second Quarter: The Teams
58-59, John W. McDonough; 60, Walter Iooss Jr.; 62, John Iacono; 63, Peter Read Miller; 64, Andy Hayt; 66, Al Tielemans; 68, Neil Leifer; 70, Neil Leifer; 72, Walter Iooss Jr.; 74, Richard Mackson; 76, Walter Iooss Jr.; 78, Jerry Wachter; 80, William Smith; 82, Robert Beck.

Halftime: The Scene
84-85, Jamie Squire/Allsport; 86, Neil Leifer; 87 top, James V. Biever; middle, Heinz Kluetmeier; bottom, Vernon J. Biever; 88 top left, John E. Biever; top right, Vernon J. Biever; bottom, Stephen Dunn/Allsport; 89 left, Vernon J. Biever; right, Andy Lyons/Allsport; 90, Neil Leifer; 91 top, Walter Iooss Jr.; middle, Vernon J. Biever; bottom, Walter Iooss Jr.; 92 top, Heinz Kluetmeier; bottom, Vernon J. Biever; 92-93, Otto Gruele/Allsport; 93, Rick Stewart; 94 top, Vernon J. Biever; bottom, Bill Frakes; 95, Vernon J. Biever; 96, Rich Clarkson; 97 top left, Al Tielemans; top right, Walter Iooss Jr.; bottom, Robert Beck.

Third Quarter: The Players
98-99, Peter Read Miller; 101, Peter Read Miller; 102, Peter Read Miller; 103 left, Walter Iooss Jr.; right, Heinz Kluetmeier; 104, Peter Read Miller; 106, Neil Leifer; 108, Heinz Kluetmeier; 110, Allan Levenson/Allsport; 112, James Drake; 115, Heinz Kluetmeier; 116, Mickey Pfleger; 118, Walter Iooss Jr.; 120 left, Heinz Kluetmeier; right, Heinz Kluetmeier; 123, Joe McNally; 124, Al Messerschmidt/NFL Photos; 126, Andy Freeberg; 128, Mike Powell/Allsport; 130, Ronald Modra; 132, Gabe Palaccio; 134, NFL Photos; 136, Peter Read Miller; 138 left, Scott Cunningham/NFL Photos; right, Vernon J. Biever; 140, Peter Read Miller; 142, Bruce Dierdorff/NFL Photos.

Fourth Quarter: The Game in Pictures
144-145, Peter Read Miller; 146, Walter Iooss Jr.; 147, Walter Iooss Jr.; 148-149, Walter Iooss Jr.; 150-151, Jerry Wachter; 151, Peter Read Miller; 152, Heinz Kluetmeier; 153 top, James Drake; bottom, Richard Mackson; 154 top, Walter Iooss Jr.; bottom, Walter Iooss Jr.; 155, Allsport USA; 156, Richard Mackson; 157, Walter Iooss Jr.; 158, Walter Iooss Jr.; 159, Walter Iooss Jr.; 160, John Iacono; 161, Walter Iooss Jr.; 162-163, Al Tielemans; 164-165, Peter Read Miller; 166-167, Walter Iooss Jr.; 168, Walter Iooss Jr.; 169, John Iacono.

Index